Robinson Township Library
Robinson, Illinois 62454

51385

O
307.7
Roy
Royston, Robert
Cities 2000.

Robinson Township Library
Robinson, Illinois 62454

CITIES 2000

McDonald's
VOUS AIDE A GARDER
VOTRE VILLE PROPRE
84, av. des Champs-Elysées
(galerie Les Champs)

CITIES 2000

Facts On File Publications
New York, New York • Bicester, England

Robinson Township Library
Robinson, Illinois 62454

This book was devised and produced by
Multimedia Publications (UK) Limited

Editor Angela Royston
Design John Strange
Production Arnon Orbach

Copyright © 1985 by Multimedia Publications (UK) Limited

First published in the United States of America by Facts On File, Inc.,
460 Park Avenue South,
New York, NY 10016

First published in Great Britain

All rights reserved. No part of this book may be reproduced or utilized
in any form or by any means, electronic or mechanical, including
photocopying, recording or by any information storage and retrieval
systems, without permission in writing from the Publisher.

Library of Congress Cataloging in Publication Data

Royston, Robert.
  Cities 2000.

  (Your world 2000)
  Includes index.
  Summary: Examines the history, growth, preservation,
and planning of cities and predicts what life will be
like in the city of the future.
  1. Cities and town. 2. City planning. 3. Urbaniza-
tion. [1. Cities and towns. 2. City planning.
3. Urbanization] I. Asimov, Isaac, 1920-
II. Title. III. Series.
HT151.P516 1985   307.7'64   84-21111
ISBN 0-8160-1154-0

Printed in Italy
10 9 8 7 6 5 4 3 2 1

CONTENTS

Foreword	6
Introduction	8
CHAPTER 1	
What is a city?	10
CHAPTER 2	
Changing cities	16
CHAPTER 3	
Planning the city	24
CHAPTER 4	
Building the city	34
CHAPTER 5	
Living in the city	42
CHAPTER 6	
2000 and beyond	52
Glossary	58
Index	62

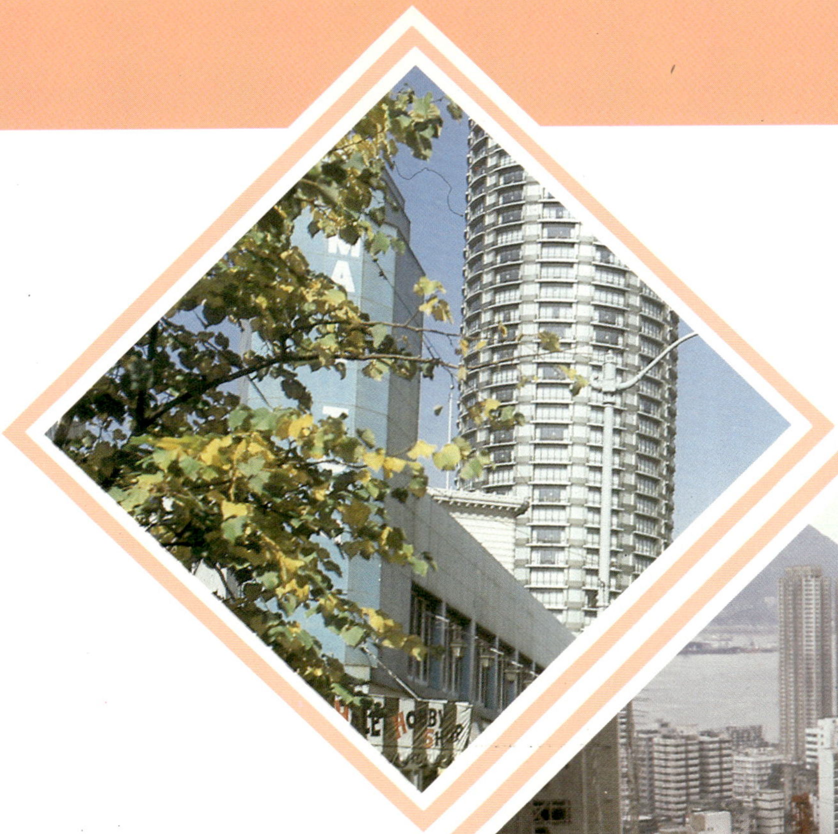

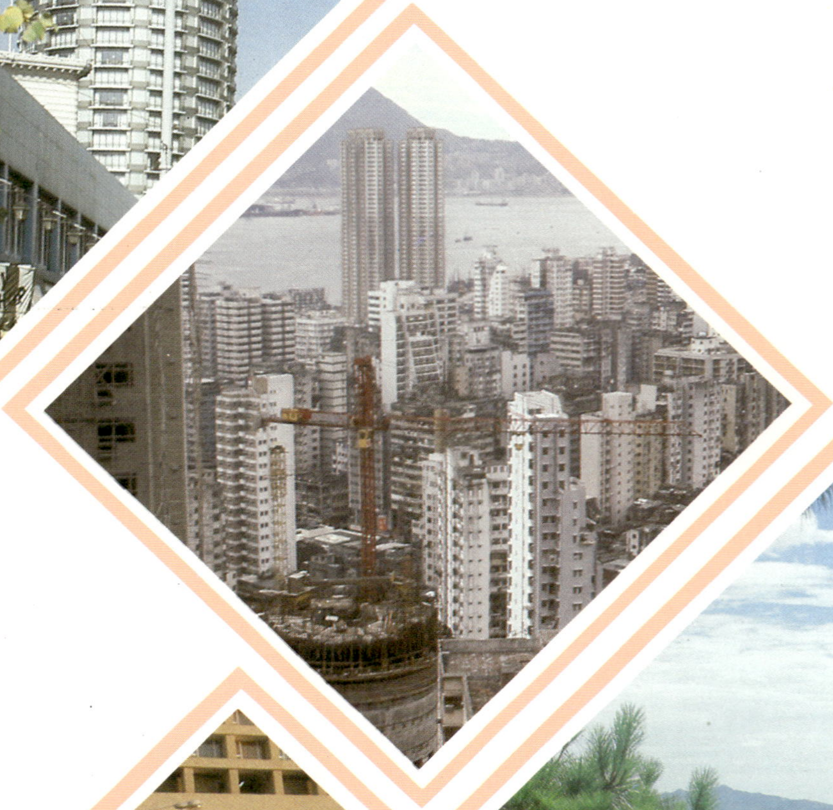

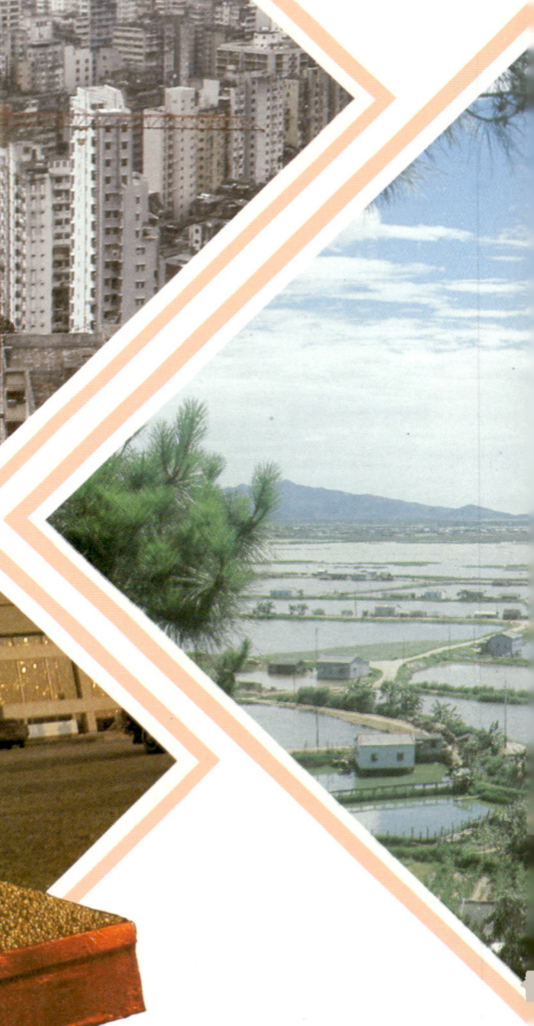

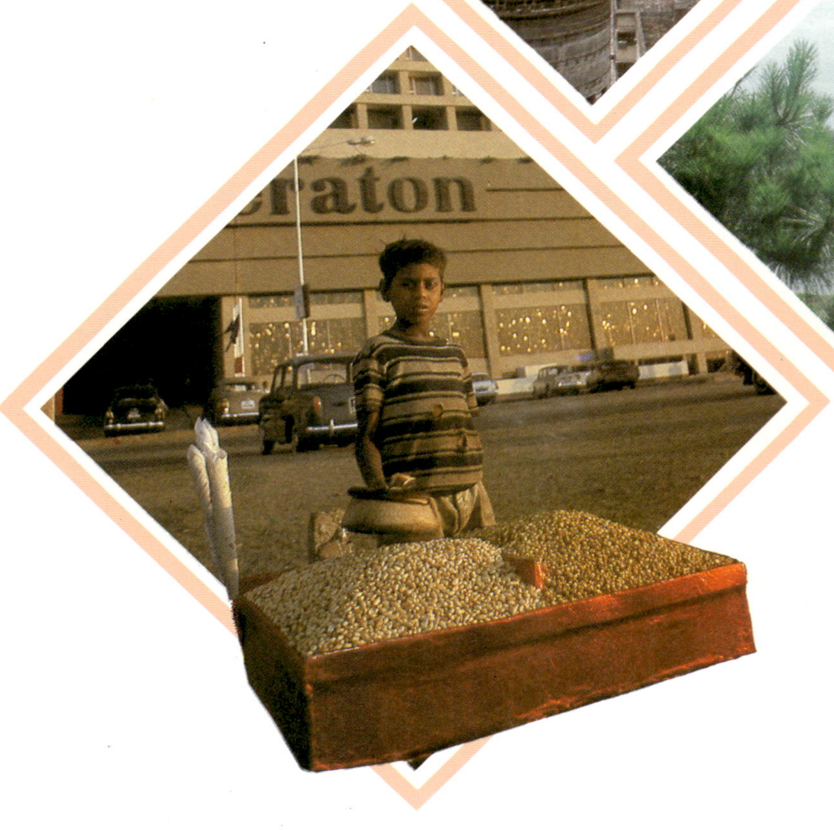
eraton

Foreword

Cities have been with us now for ten thousand years, though at the start they were very small and primitive. However, even small and primitive cities have always held people closely together. In cities, people talked with each other, interacted, developed their ideas, and in general advanced more quickly than people living in isolation or in small groups.

The city-dwellers themselves always felt 'advanced' and always had a high opinion of themselves. It was in the cities that culture moved forward most rapidly and it was there that new and supposedly better ways originated. The city-dwellers even controlled the development of the language and used it to praise themselves.

The Greek word for city is *polis*. The behaviour of a city-dweller is 'polite'. He has 'polished' manners. These became complimentary words that could not be applied to countrymen. Countrymen worked in the fields of country villas, so they were 'villeins'. The Teutonic word for a farmer is *Bauer* or *Boer*, so countrymen are 'boors'. These are *not* complimentary words.

The Latin word for 'city' is *urbs*, so city-dwellers are 'urbane'. A later Latin word for 'city' was *civitas*, so city-dwellers are 'civil' and 'civilized'. The word 'civilization' comes from the same root.

Through most of history, city-dwellers were a small minority of humanity, and considered themselves an elite. About two hundred years ago, however, cities began to grow as more and more people flocked into them. Cities are *still* growing, and more rapidly than ever, and they have changed greatly in the process. The opportunities in cities, the excitement – and the problems – have increased enormously. By 2000, half the people in the world will be living in cities, some of them containing as many as 30 million people.

What will life be like in such cities? That is what this book will tell you.

Isaac Asimov

Introduction

The cities of 2000 and beyond are already taking shape. How will they look? Will they have mile-high buildings cutting the sky, or, as recently built skyscrapers are blown up, will new houses look more like the terraces and squares built a century ago? Inside the home there will be many changes. As electricity and gas become more expensive, computers will control heating, lighting and cooking to use energy as efficiently as possible. Videos will bring more entertainment into the home and many families will have a computer to link them directly with shops, offices and banks. This book looks at these possibilities and many others. New systems of transport will include people-movers, shared vehicles and short take-off and land airports close to city centres. Some cities are declining in population, leaving desolate inner-city areas ripe for new ideas. Other cities in Africa and South America are growing so fast they are dwarfing many of the industrial giants of today and yesterday. What problems will these megacities have to cope with in AD 2000?

Author: **Robert Royston** is a freelance journalist and writer who has written many books for children. His particular interests are history and current affairs.

Consultant: **David Satterthwaite,** researcher on Human Settlements Programme, International Institute for Environment and Development.

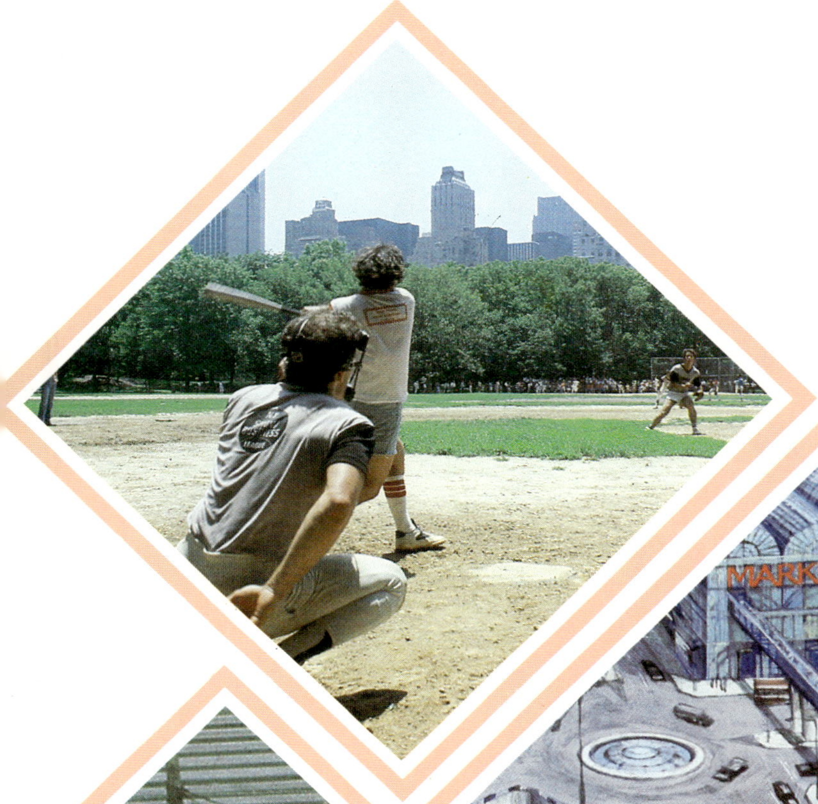

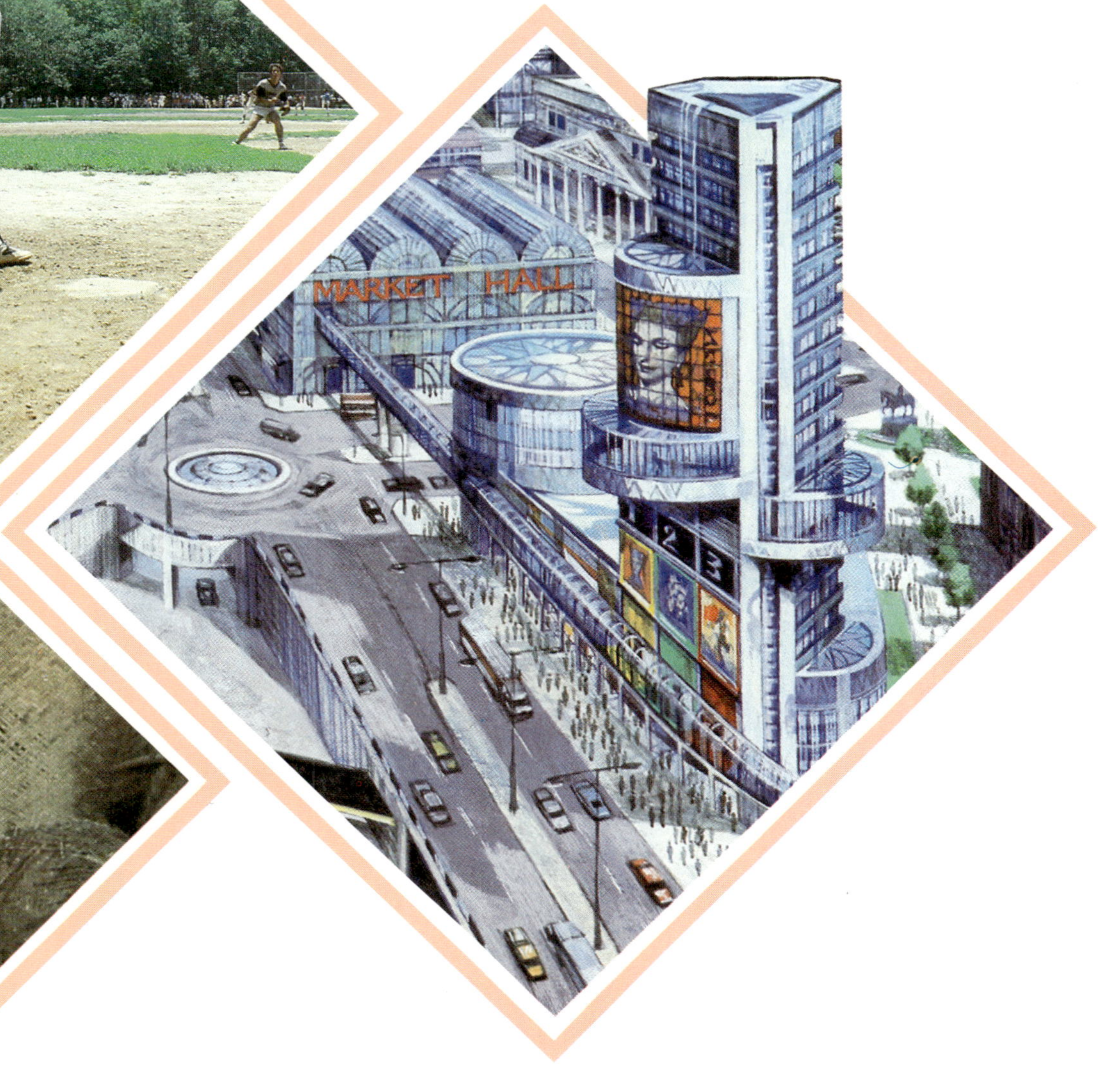

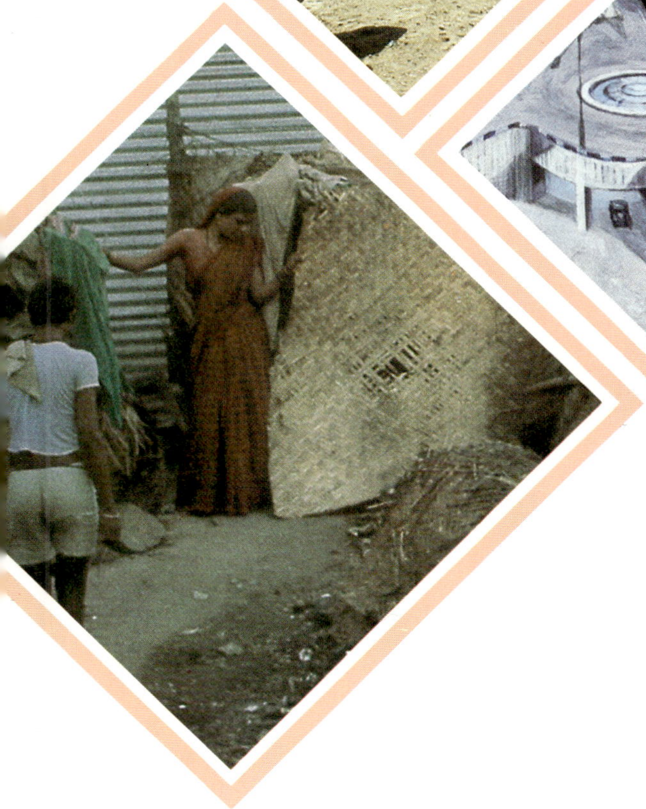

CHAPTER 1
What is a city?

This is a book about cities, their past and their life in the present. But particularly it is about where cities are going and what they may be like in the year 2000 and beyond.

For more than five thousand years only a tiny proportion of the world's population lived in cities. Then at the end of the 18th century cities began to grow and change rapidly. At the end of the last century, 15 per cent of the world's population lived in urban settlements. In 1980 the figure was 41.2 per cent. By AD 2000 it will be 50.1 per cent, a staggering 3000 to 3500 million people. The biggest city will probably be Mexico City with 31 million people.

All this adds up to terrific change in a very short space of time. Behind it lies another change. Goods used to be produced mainly in the countryside, but now they are produced mainly in cities.

Life in cities
People live in cities because they were born and brought up there, or because they came off the land looking for more work and money and excitement. On the land they did not rely much on others. They produced their own food, built their own houses and made their own tools and clothes. In cities everyone relies on other people for most of the things they need.

Take a typical city dweller. Let's make him or her an office worker. She could live in any big city from Lima in Peru to Milan in Italy, from Bombay in India to Boston in the United States. When she gets up in the morning and switches on the lights and makes her breakfast, she relies on power workers to supply electricity. Her news is brought to her on the radio and in a newspaper by broadcasters and journalists.

A bus driver gets her to work in a bus which is serviced by mechanics and organized by people who run the whole transport service. If the street cleaners have done their jobs, our office worker will not find the streets filthy.

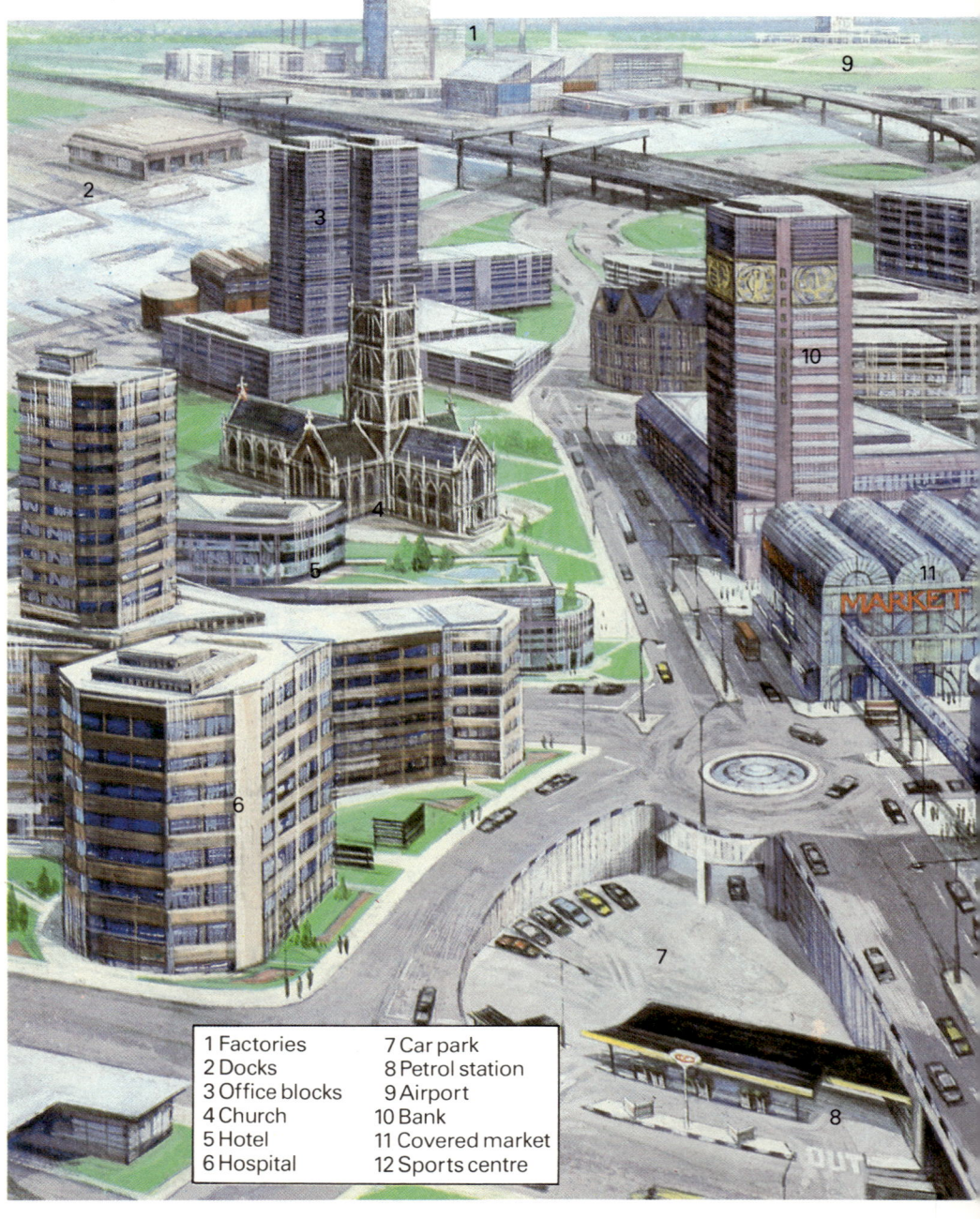

In the office, managers run the organization she works for. Suppose it is a company which makes shoes. Executives decide how many shoes of each kind are made in the factories. Truck drivers take the goods from the factories to the warehouses, and from the warehouses to the shops for sale. In the office there are also clerks and secretaries, telephone operators and a sales staff.

Private and public sectors
In most countries there are two sections of industry. One is private. Business people use their own money, or money borrowed from banks, to start and run factories, companies or shops. The other is public. The State uses money from taxes to run industries such as ship building, coal mining, or steel production.

In communist countries the

1 Factories	7 Car park
2 Docks	8 Petrol station
3 Office blocks	9 Airport
4 Church	10 Bank
5 Hotel	11 Covered market
6 Hospital	12 Sports centre

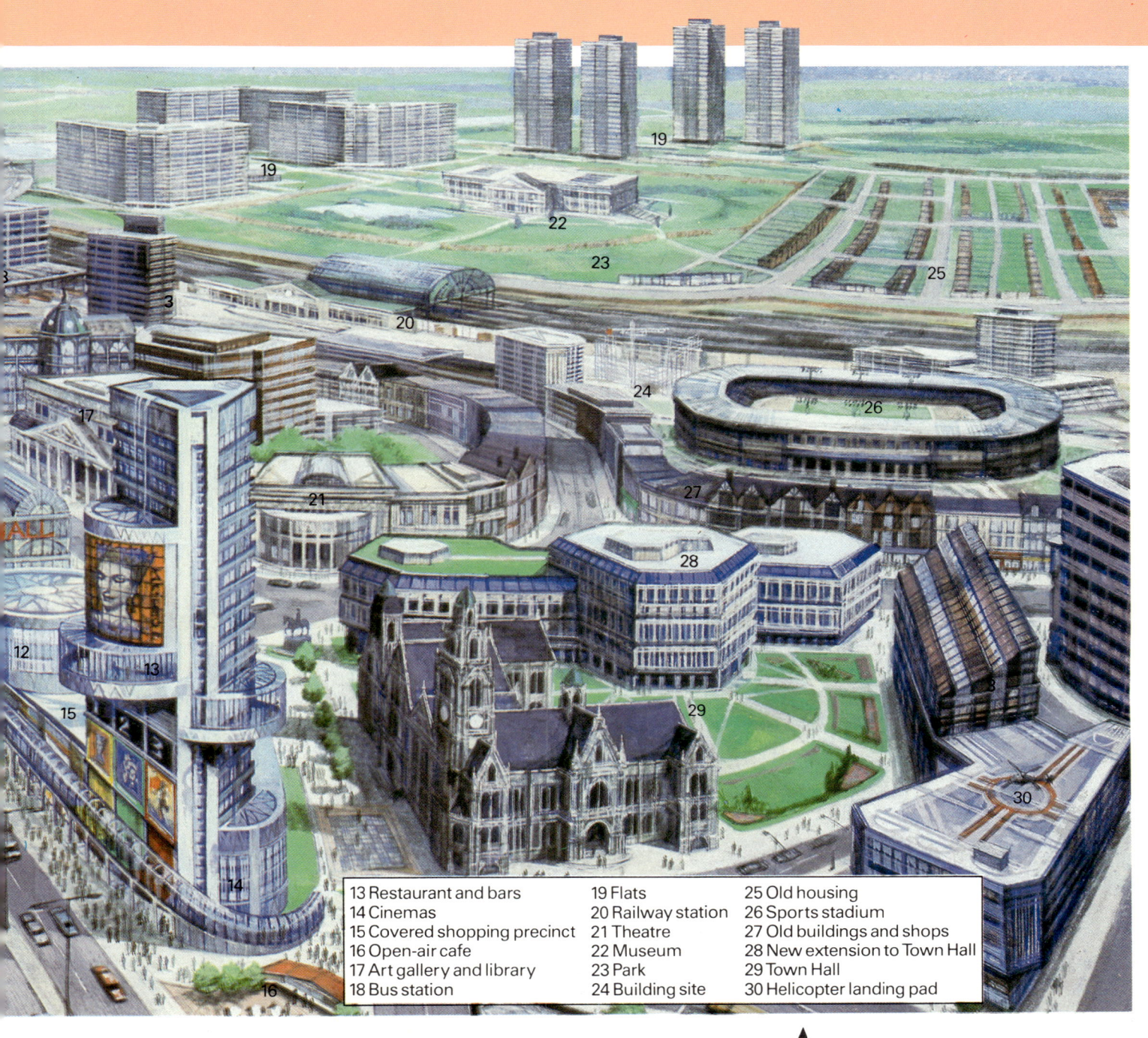

13 Restaurant and bars	19 Flats	25 Old housing
14 Cinemas	20 Railway station	26 Sports stadium
15 Covered shopping precinct	21 Theatre	27 Old buildings and shops
16 Open-air cafe	22 Museum	28 New extension to Town Hall
17 Art gallery and library	23 Park	29 Town Hall
18 Bus station	24 Building site	30 Helicopter landing pad

private sector is either not allowed or strictly controlled. They believe that the private businessman's wish for profits for himself is bad for society.

City government
Many decisions have to be taken in the running of a city. Should a new road go here or there? If it goes there it may cause traffic to block up another road somewhere else. Should more garbage collectors be employed? These and other questions are decided by city councils. Often there is a central council and local neighbourhood councils who decide on day-to-day matters.

Other services that are essential to cities, such as hospitals or schools and universities, are often run by special committees responsible to departments of the central government.

Cities get money by charging taxes on property and buildings. Some put a tax on many other things such as certain activities or types of work or certain goods sold. More money is put into the city by the central government who gets it mainly by taxing people on their incomes.

▲ The busy centre of a modern city. People come into the centre to work, shop and enjoy themselves. They travel in by bus, train or car. Some buildings are old, some are new. Will tomorrow's cities be very different?

11

Supplying the city

Cities are centres of work and industry, but they cannot create everything they require. Many urgently needed things must be brought into the city including food, fuel, manufactured goods, water and energy.

Energy
Electricity creates light and heat, and supplies power which is used to run industrial machines. Household gadgets such as washing machines and vacuum cleaners also run on electricity.

It is produced in power stations which are often miles from the city. Fuels such as coal or oil are burned to create steam. This drives a machine called a turbine-generator, which makes electricity. Nuclear power is also used to generate electricity. In the future more electricity may be made from sunlight, or hydrogen fusion, or from the power of wind or waves, or by using falling water or water in a dam to drive the turbine-generator.

Electricity passes from the power station along wires to the city where transformers receive it. They lower the strength and then change it into different types of charge suitable for offices, homes or factories.

Cities need transport – cars, trucks and buses, which run on petrol or diesel oil. These are made from crude oil, brought up from under the ground or seabed. Oil is transported through huge pipelines, or across the sea in special tankers. After being unloaded in ports and refined, it is brought to cities by huge trucks. It is burned for heat as well as to produce electricity.

Gas, which is used for cooking or heating is extracted from under the ground or seabed, or made from coal. The first form is called natural gas and the second town or coal gas.

Water
Water for our cities comes from lakes, rivers or wells. It is stored in reservoirs, but, before it is used, it is purified to make it safe to drink. Then it is piped to other reservoirs. These are built in high places so the water flows down the pipes creating pressure. This is why water comes out of the tap when you turn it on.

Food
A tiny quantity of food is grown in cities in gardens, allotments or even on the roofs of buildings, where a method called hydroponics is used. But most of what we eat comes from farms

here or in other countries. Trucks and trains bring food to markets where it is bought by butchers, grocers and greengrocers who sell it to the public. Food from other countries is brought to us by sea, road and rail and sometimes by air. Meat particularly must be frozen to prevent it from going rotten if it comes from abroad.

We shall see on pages 18 and 19 that the cities of the Third World are growing fast. Feeding them is a huge problem that will become more and more urgent as the year 2000 comes closer. The best way to feed the hungry is by farming crops. Land which produces 6.5 lb (3 kilograms) of meat can produce 88 lb (40 kilograms) of cereals. But rich countries want meat and so farmers produce it because they are paid better for doing so. The hungry stay hungry in cities like Lagos and Calcutta.

Another problem is that cereals are not such a good source of protein as meat. But beans, or beans mixed with cereals, can provide enough protein. Again, though, most farmers want to sell meat to the rich cities.

Fish farming may become a more important method of food production after AD 2000. Eggs are removed from the fish, hatched, and the young are kept in enclosed areas of the sea. This can produce a rich harvest of fish at low cost.

Communications

We rely on newspapers and radio or television reports to tell us what is happening in the world. Cities are linked up all over the world by telephones and satellites.

Much of the business of the richer cities is done by phone. In the year 2000 and beyond we shall not only speak to people in other cities but see pictures of them on a screen. We may hold meetings across the world, each seeing everyone else on his or her own screen.

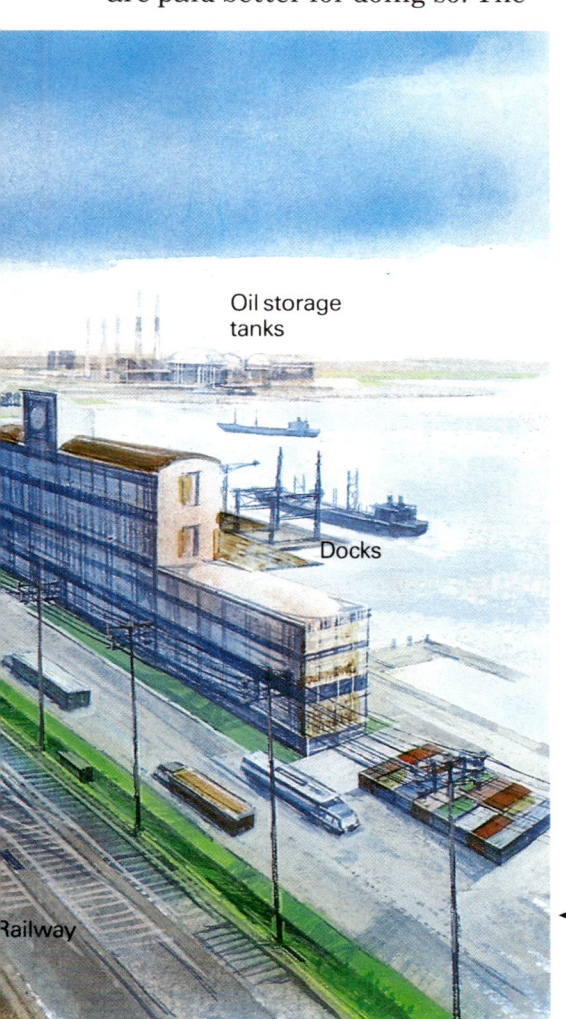

◀ A city uses vast quantities of electricity, gas, water, food, raw materials and goods. A city also produces many things. Trucks, trains, ships and planes take goods and people to and from the city.

▲ Stores buy food from farmers in special markets. It is then sold to us in city shops and stores. This early morning market is Spitalfields, London.

Each day New York uses:	
Water	1 000 000 000 gal
	(3 800 000 000 litres)
Food	
vegetables	5 200 000 lb
	(2 400 000 kg)
meat	2 700 000 lb
	(1 200 000 lb)
poultry	1 300 000 lb
	(600 000 kg)
eggs	108 000 000
Energy	
electricity	2600 megawatt hrs
oil	5 500 000 gallons
	(21 000 000 litres)

▼ Fish farming may provide much food for hungry cities in the future. This farm will provide fish for people in Hong Kong.

Removing the waste

If all the garbage produced by a big city was piled up, it would soon look like a range of mountains. Newspapers, bottles, boxes, cans, potato peels, chicken bones, old cars, broken chairs, wrecked television sets are just some of the things you would find in the heap. Then there is waste produced by factories, as well as human waste, which is carried away by sewers under the city streets.

What to do with all this has been a problem for centuries. But garbage could soon be considered less of a problem and more of a benefit because people have begun to see how valuable it is.

Throughout history three solutions to the garbage problem have been used. One is to throw it in the streets, another is to dump it all in special areas, and a third is to re-use it. As metals, paper and glass become more expensive, the third solution will become more important.

In ancient Troy people simply threw their rubbish outside the front door. It piled up in the street and the smell was terrible. Occasionally people would lay

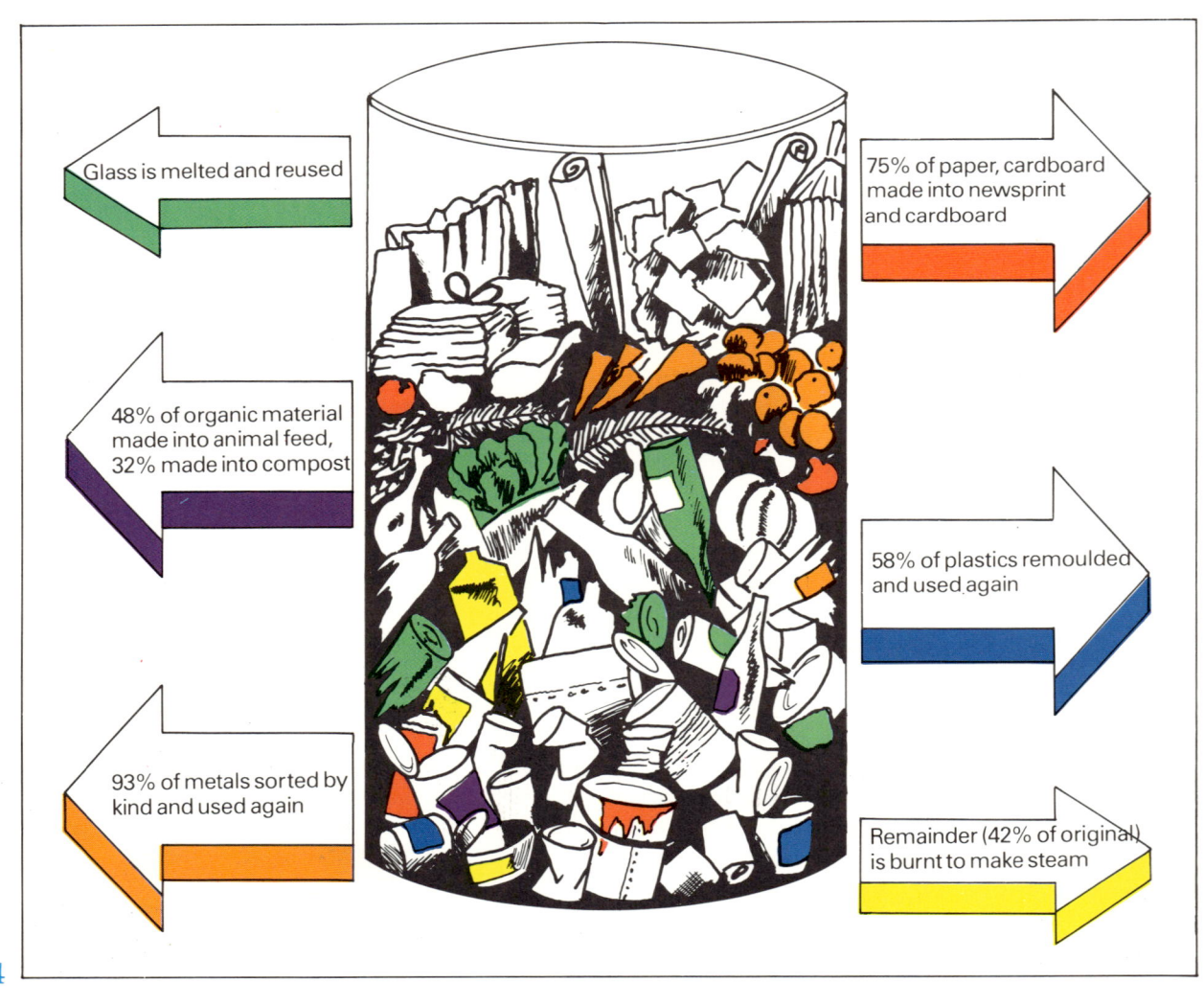

▲ Garbage collectors in Cairo. A group of about 40,000 people, called the Zabaleen, collect trash from richer Cairo homes. They sort out articles they can re-use or sell, and, in this way, earn a lot of money themselves.

▼ Sorting out a city's garbage to save that which can be re-used is a complicated process. This diagram shows how much metal, glass, and other things Rome manages to re-use.

- Glass is melted and reused
- 75% of paper, cardboard made into newsprint and cardboard
- 48% of organic material made into animal feed, 32% made into compost
- 58% of plastics remoulded and used again
- 93% of metals sorted by kind and used again
- Remainder (42% of original) is burnt to make steam

14

▶ New York and Cairo have about the same number of people living in them. New York's inhabitants produce more of the kind of rubbish that can be re-used.

fresh clay over it all. Every so often people had to rebuild their houses because the ground around them was rising by four feet (over a metre) a year.

In modern times most household garbage is collected from bins outside houses. Much of it is then taken to incinerators and burned. Often it is used to fill in weak or pitted ground to make the land suitable for building on. Factory waste and human waste was, and often still is, pumped into rivers or the sea.

The old ways of getting rid of garbage are now strongly criticized on two grounds – they are dangerous, and they destroy something that could be valuable. Waste in the sea and rivers damages natural life there. And when some factories burn garbage before dumping it, the chimneys belch poisonous smoke into the atmosphere.

Clean air laws threatened factories with fines if their smoke was dirty. An American company called Westvaco then realized it could extract the paper and pulp which made its waste so dangerous to burn. This was turned into chemicals which were sold. A whole new branch of the business was formed.

Recycling garbage
Many other things besides chemicals can be made from waste. Discarded food, like bones and skin, can be taken out and made into cattle feed. It is a quarter the price of the grain usually fed to animals. Metal and bottles can be sorted out, melted down and re-used.

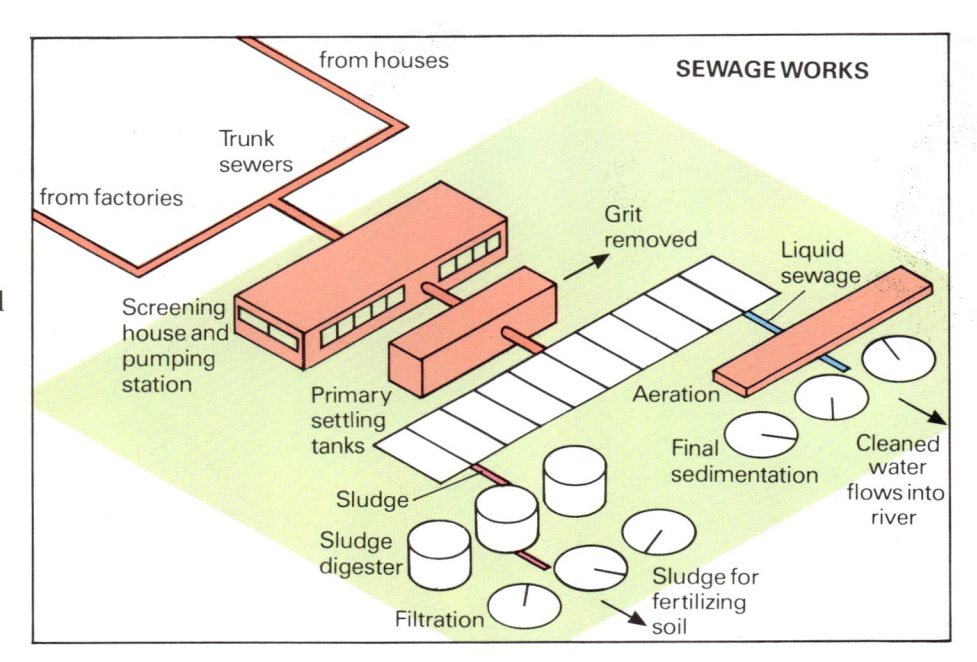

Some countries encourage people to do the sorting themselves by not throwing certain things out in the general garbage. Switzerland has planned neighbourhood bottle bins with different containers for different coloured bottles. In Oregon in the United States shopkeepers have to pay back a deposit when you return cans or bottles which held soft drinks or beer. But you get more money back on the sort of bottles that can be re-used.

Newspapers and cans are also valuable. But people will not

▲ A sewage farm uses bacteria to clean the water from the sewers. The water does not cause pollution and the left-over sewage can be used as fertilizer.

save them for re-use unless governments encourage them to do so.

Sewage farms
Human waste need not pollute rivers and the sea. Sewage farms filter and clean the water so that it can be used again. The remaining excrement is treated and can be used as fertilizer. Sewage farms can be expensive to set up, but cheaper in the long run than polluting and destroying whole rivers and areas of the sea.

CHAPTER 2
Changing cities

Cities have changed more in the last 200 years than in the previous 5000. The first cities in Mesopotamia were tiny, with populations of 2000 or less. No one then could have dreamed that today we can build skyscrapers in a few months and have to fight to preserve the countryside against the march of roads and concrete.

What caused this sudden spurt of growth and what caused the earliest tiny villages to become cities thousands of years ago?

When farming was developed in Mesopotamia 10 000 years ago, enough food could be grown for the small population.

People then began to build more permanent houses and to make and sell utensils and decorative objects. As more was produced so trade spread between different areas. Cities became centres of trade. People came to these growing cities looking for work and to be part of life in settlements that now boasted squares, monuments, fine houses and sometimes palaces and temples.

A wish for power and wealth affected the history and growth of early cities. For example, a

▲ The ancient Sumerian city of Ur was captured by the warrior Sargon and included in his empire. Ur was a wealthy city with many religious monuments and palaces. It was near the Euphrates river and on a main trade route. The photograph shows the remains of the magnificent ziggurat of Ur.

▶ A London slum in 1878. The Industrial Revolution brought more work to many cities, but also smoke, filth and poverty. Factories and houses were built side by side, making living conditions dirty and unhealthy.

▶▶ As city roads and railways improved, people moved out of the city centre to the spreading suburbs. People wanted to get away from the smoke to houses with gardens like this.

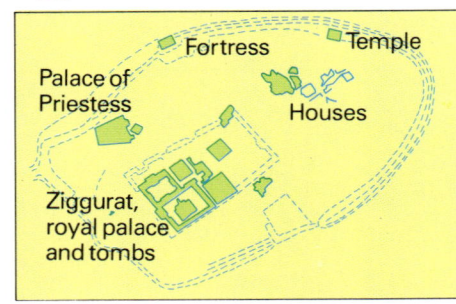

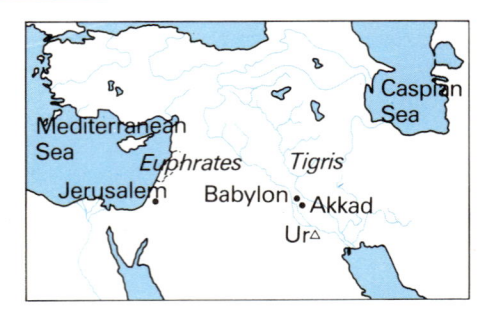

military conqueror called Sargon rose to a position of power in the royal court of Kish in Mesopotamia in 2400 BC. He then started his own city, called Akkad, and conquered Ur and many others from Anatolia to the Persian Gulf, capturing slaves and controlling trade routes. Akkad became the powerful capital of a large empire.

Later, people came to cities because important new ideas were formed there. In Athens thinkers and playwrights created works which laid the foundations for much of today's science and art. In Rome ideas to do with government and law were formed.

Barbarian invaders left most of the ancient cities in ruins. But new cities arose, especially in medieval times when trade between nations and between European centres and the East began. Cities with ports were well placed for trade and some, like Antwerp, Bruges and London grew in wealth and power.

▶ The map shows how big London was at different times in history. It grew enormously after the Industrial Revolution (see the city in 1900) and even more since then as more and more suburbs and New Towns have been built around London.

The Industrial Revolution
Cities changed little until the Industrial Revolution of the 18th, 19th and 20th centuries. James Watt's steam engine used steam from coal to drive machines. This engine was one of the first of many which allowed huge numbers of goods to be made by machine instead of a few by hand.

Industries grew up in cities and around the coalfields. Some whole new cities grew up around new industry. People flocked to the cities for work. Industrial growth made London, already the capital of a huge empire, the world's largest seaport, and also the centre of a railway network across all of Britain. London's population, over a million in 1820, reached 6.6 million by 1900.

At first there were no laws governing living and working conditions. People lived in filthy overcrowded rooms. There was little clean water and no sewers.

Then the inventions of the Industrial Revolution began to transform the cities in another way. As the table shows, many of the things we take for granted today – light bulbs, trains, the motor car – did not exist before the 19th century.

Crowded, dirty and unhealthy conditions at the centre made people move out. New, faster trains and buses allowed them to create suburbs where the air was fresh and there were trees and gardens. Old country villages were swallowed up by the spreading suburbs.

The making of modern cities
New inventions continue. Skyscrapers have been vital to modern cities where space is scarce. But they could not have been built before the discovery of new building materials, or before elevators (lifts), air conditioning and methods of ventilation had been invented.

The latest phase of the Industrial Revolution is in computers and this will have a big effect on our lives by 2000, as we shall see on pages 44 and 45.

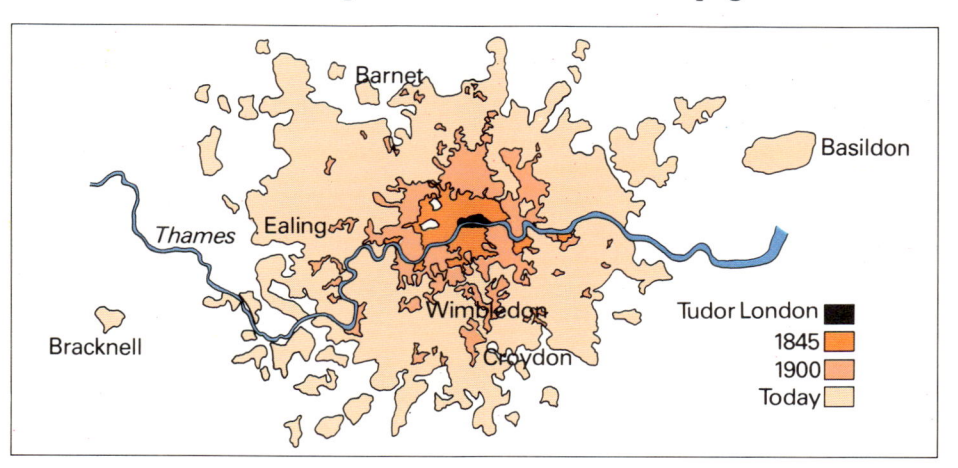

Tudor London ■
1845 ■
1900 ■
Today □

Inventions
1804 Steam locomotive
1853 Passenger elevator (lift)
1858 Refrigerator
1858 Washing machine
1859 Internal combustion engine
1867 Typewriter
1876 Telephone
1879 Edison's electric lamp
1887 Gramophone
1887 Motor car engine
1895 Wireless telegraphy
1889 Flush toilet
1899 Tape recorder
1901 Vacuum cleaner
1903 Aeroplane
1915 Tungsten filament lamp
1925 Television
1925 Frozen food process
1956 Videotape recording
1959 Microwave oven
1960 Laser
1965 Holography

Growing cities

Many European and American cities grew frantically during the Industrial Revolution. Today, most of the old industrial cities have slowed down or stopped growing, and cities in Africa, Asia and Latin America have taken over as the front runners.

These huge new cities are doubling their population every twelve years, twice as fast as in 19th century Europe. By the year 2000 only New York will represent the old industrial cities in the list of the ten biggest cities. Mexico City will probably be the biggest, its population having jumped from 2.7 million in 1950 to 31 million.

Today just over half the world's city dwellers live in the poor countries of the Third World. By AD 2000 two thirds of them will live there. Most of these mainly southern nations were once the colonies of advanced European countries and many have little industry. There is already terrible overcrowding, slums, poverty and disease in Third World cities. In the next century these conditions will be worse as we will see on pages 21 and 22.

Causes of Third World growth
Natural population growth is very rapid in much of the Third World. Poor people there have always had large families, but epidemics which in the past killed huge numbers of people are now prevented by modern drugs. People collected together in cities are easier to treat than people scattered across the land. The death rate in many Third World cities has been halved in the last few decades.

Increased supplies of food increase the rate at which the population grows. Cities expand too because they attract people looking for work. Most rural people migrate to cities not because they want to but because they have to.

Drought, disease and the world shortage of firewood have made life on the land impossible in some areas. And some big landowners force many of their poorer tenants to leave their farms. Peasants then have to try their luck in city slums rather than live on the brink of starvation. But it is not only work they are looking for.

They come looking for better health care. Town dwellers in India for example have a nine times better chance of good medical attention than their brothers and sisters on the land. The figure is eleven times in Ghana and thirty-three times in Ethiopia.

The hope of better education lures people to cities. There are many more schools, colleges and training centres in urban areas. They not only attract people off the land but prevent them from returning, by training them for city work.

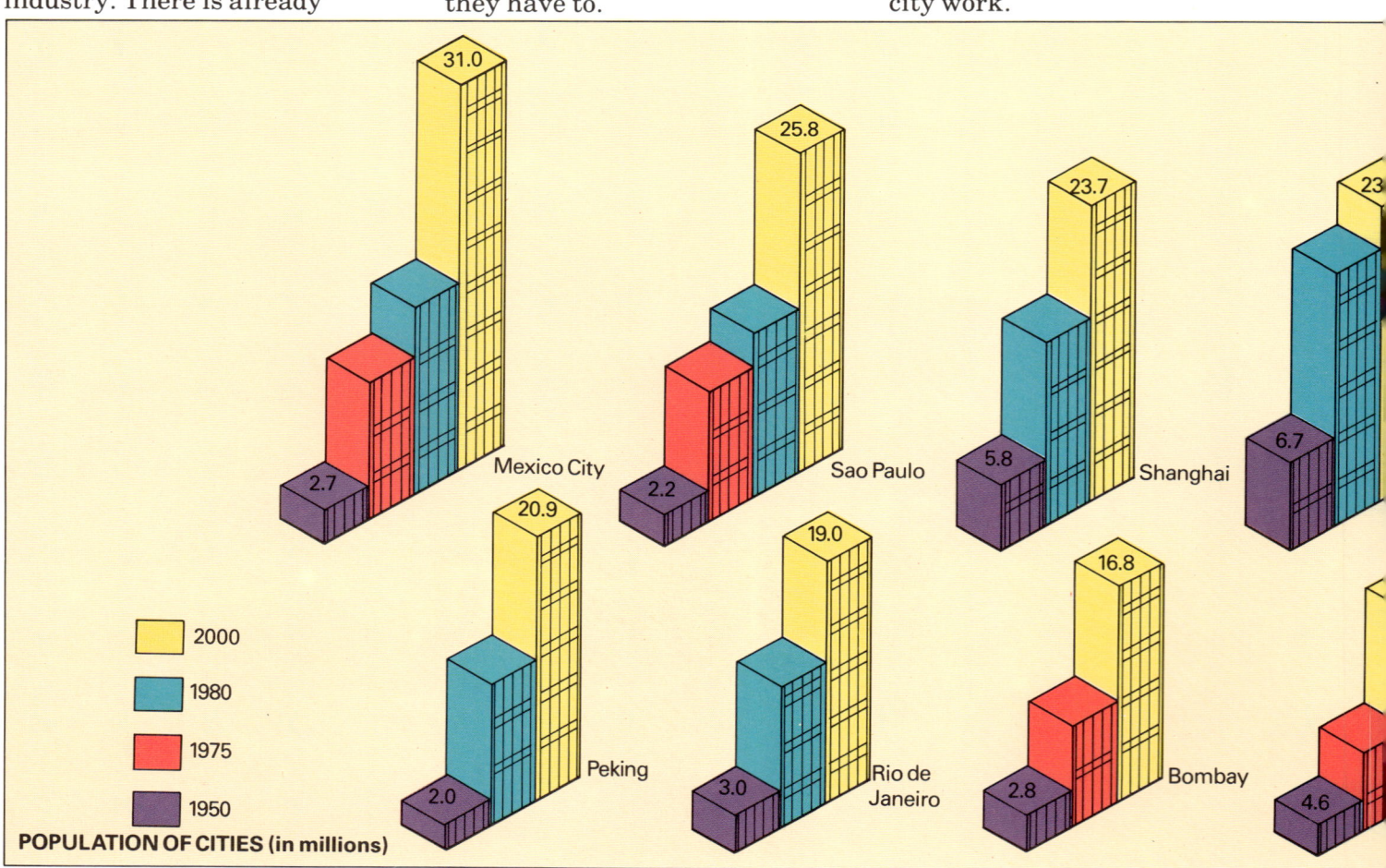

POPULATION OF CITIES (in millions)

- 2000
- 1980
- 1975
- 1950

Mexico City: 2.7 → 31.0
Sao Paulo: 2.2 → 25.8
Shanghai: 5.8 → 23.7
(6.7, 23)
Peking: 2.0 → 20.9
Rio de Janeiro: 3.0 → 19.0
Bombay: 2.8 → 16.8
(4.6)

People come looking for work and if they do not find it in offices and factories they make a living the best way they can – by selling in the streets, cleaning cars or begging.

Money for cities
Big cities grow bigger in the Third World because of the way government money is used there. A lot of government money is spent in the main cities, often just in the capital. Private businesses, too, prefer to set up in the already-large cities.

Smaller towns and villages and poor farmers on the land get much less government help, often none at all. In Bangladesh 82 per cent of working people live in rural areas, but only 10 per cent of government financial aid is spent there. Farmers get poorer and a move to the city looks increasingly attractive.

The developed world sends some aid to poorer countries. Part of this aid may be surplus food produced in Europe or North America. This extra food causes a fall in local prices so farmers get less for what they have produced. In future, Third World governments will be strongly advised to invest more in the rural areas.

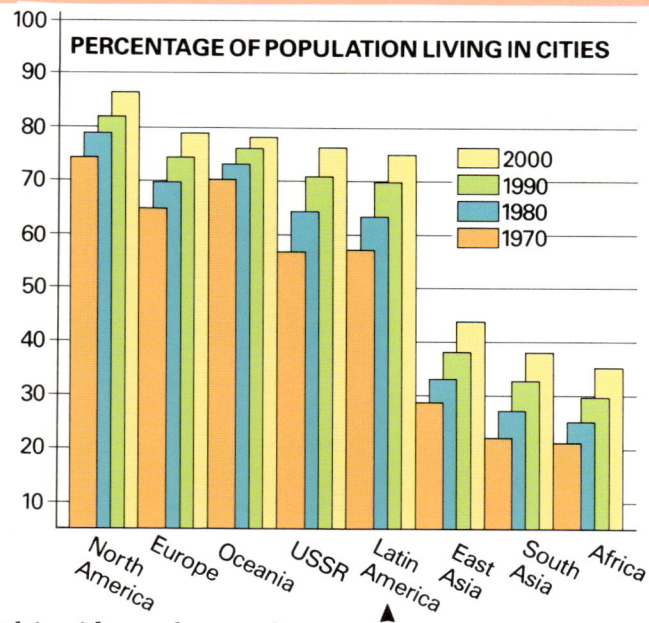

PERCENTAGE OF POPULATION LIVING IN CITIES (2000, 1990, 1980, 1970) — North America, Europe, Oceania, USSR, Latin America, East Asia, South Asia, Africa

▲ Latin America is the only Third World region where a high percentage of the population lives in cities. In this, it is like Europe and North America.

◀ By the year 2000 these ten cities will be at the top of the population league. New York is the only old industrial city which will keep up with the new leaders.

▼ Many poor people in the Third World cannot make enough to survive from farming. They leave the land and their small villages and come to the city to look for work.

Tokyo-Yokohama 22.4 — New York — Calcutta 12.3 — Jakarta 15.7 — 2.6

The new megacities

The growth of Third World urban centres into megacities (city giants) will not stop or even slow down much in the foreseeable future. So, as the year 2000 draws closer, how will they cope with the extra millions? This is one of the most important problems facing us. To make matters worse a lot of the new populations of Third World cities live in slums and are among the poorest people of all on Earth.

Shanty towns

Around cities such as Lagos, Rio de Janiero and Calcutta, shanty towns have grown huge. People live here who cannot afford to live anywhere else. They build shelters of mud, wood or stone, or of whatever is to hand – junk, tin, even cardboard.

The shanty towns have become 'misery villages' with no clean water for drinking or cooking, and no proper health care or waste removal. The rotting garbage in the streets attracts flies, rats and diseases like typhoid and dysentry. The areas smell terrible. Malnutrition is common because work is hard to get and food, therefore, scarce. Because the shanty towns are illegal, the cities they grow up around have no responsibility for helping them. At the same time they realize they cannot go on ignoring them.

No government help

In many Third World cities shanty towns house up to a third or even a half of the population. They are often growing twice as fast as the rest of the city. Governments and city councils must plan quickly to avoid more misery and disaster. But most have not done so and shanty town problems are getting worse. Shanty towns also bring more problems to the whole city – and these cities had plenty of problems to begin with.

As more and more people come into or are born in the megacities, overcrowding becomes worse. People looking for work, or peddling articles for sale, jam the streets. Water supplies are threatened by the ever increasing demand. More use of electricity causes regular power failures in some cities. Factories drill their own wells and use their own generators when the city's electricity supply fails. Buses and trains cannot cope with the growing load. Overcrowding in apartments as well as in shanty towns gets worse.

Solutions?

What are nations to do? So far a common 'solution' has been to

◀ Poor people who cannot afford city rents build their own homes in shanty towns, using whatever materials they can find.

bulldoze the illegal shanty towns. This has proved to be a big mistake. It does not create housing but destroys it, and the shanty dwellers do not just go away. Next day they start rebuilding their shelters.

Governments have been advised to accept the shanty towns and provide city services, particularly piped water and rubbish and sewage removal. This would cut down disease. Also governments have been urged to help people build their own houses or improve existing shacks and huts. They may do this by providing simple and cheap building materials. Some countries have done this, and bulldozing is now more rare.

Poor world
We must remember that these problems are caused by the fact that Third World countries are poor. One reason for this is that the Industrial Revolution did not lead to the poor countries developing their own industries. Instead they supplied raw materials for the rich world's factories and helped the rich get richer, as we shall see on pages 56 and 57.

We must also remember that people come off the land to share in the opportunity and excitement of city life. They expect a higher living standard and often get it. Despite dreadful conditions many shanty dwellers prefer life there. In the slums some visitors from the developed world have seen a community spirit they say is not easy to find elsewhere.

▲ A child selling peanuts outside the Sheraton Hotel in Bombay, India. Work is hard to find in the megacities and everyone has to make a living as best they can.

▼ A carnival in Olinda in Brazil. Street festivals are a part of life in many poor cities.

Old cities

The absence of shanty towns in Europe and America should not lead us to believe that cities there have no problems. The slums in the industrial inner cities are poor and desolate places, where crime, violence, unemployment and alcoholism are rife. They are not as bad as Third World shanty towns but living conditions in them are often grim and unhealthy. How they can be helped is an urgent question today and will not get less urgent as 2000 approaches.

The inner city
The inner city is often the old industrial area of town near the centre where a lot of growth took place during the Industrial Revolution. In those days factories may have thrived here, but today activity has often moved away. These inner city areas began to decline when richer people moved out, often to suburban neighbourhoods free from noise and grime.

An attempt to wipe out certain slums was made in Britain after World War 2 when people were moved to better homes and slum housing was flattened. But this has not solved the problem. The rate at which inner city areas became slums was speeded up by ruthless landlords, particularly in the 1950s and 60s.

They bought slum houses cheaply and crowded them with as many tenants as they could fit in. Because they were only interested in the money they could make, they spent nothing on repairs. They forced people out of other houses so they could buy them too. Often rents began low, but then rose. Soon neighbourhoods which mixed poor with not-so-poor became total slums where only desperate people were willing to live.

Because slums are poor, city councils get little money from them in taxes. Less money is spent on them as a result.

▲ The Bronx in New York is an inner city area which has been left to decay. Houses are burned down and crime and vandalism are common. The city will have to spend very large sums of money to make this area a good place to live again.

▼ The meat and vegetable markets of both London and Paris have been moved out of the city centres. What has happened to the old sites? Les Halles in Paris was torn down and this exciting new complex was built for shops, libraries and art galleries. The contrast between the old and the new is quite spectacular.

◀ Old and new exist side by side in this North American city.

In this way houses may be saved, but it is no solution. If poorer people are driven out they will merely go somewhere else. The problem is not housing but poverty. There will always be slums while there are very poor people. Tackling the problem means less money spent on rich areas and more on the inner city. Are we willing to make the sacrifice?

Changing industry
Some cities grew up around particular industries. If these industries fail the towns become areas of mass unemployment. One such area is the River Clyde in Scotland, home of a once-thriving ship-building industry. When this collapsed an already poor area became poorer still.

The dockland area of the Thames in London closed down when ships began to carry their cargo in special containers. These were easier to unload further down the river, at Tilbury. The former docks have been idle for nearly twenty years, as they wait for the city to plan a new use for them or the land they stand on.

Saving poor areas
A neighbourhood's fortunes can change. People with money may be attracted to poor areas because they want to buy houses cheaply and repair them. New offices or shopping centres may be sited close by and make former slums desirable again. Or people are attracted to historic houses which suggest an earlier time in the life of the city.

Cracks in the city
Old cities have to be repaired when roads, sewers and water pipes built for a smaller population many years ago begin to collapse. Water pipes in some areas are clogging up with the deposits that chalky water leaves behind. As the pressure of the water is increased to force it through the narrowing pipes, the pipes burst, flooding the streets with water.

◀ In Covent Garden in London, the old market buildings were kept much as they were, and the shops and restaurants have moved into them.

CHAPTER 3
Planning the city

The last chapter looked at the problems facing today's cities. Tomorrow's cities are already being planned. Will the planners be able to make our cities better places to live in?

Even in the busiest parts of cities we want as much light and clean air as possible. We want some open spaces too, and, in places, peace and quiet. None of this would occur if we did not plan our cities. It is not often possible to do this from the start. But we can certainly plan new neighbourhoods and control the way old ones change. In the year 2000, city planners are likely to take more notice of what people want out of city life than they have in the past.

City design

Planners usually have to work within the cities that already exist. They are limited by the layout of the city and its streets. Most cities have streets that are built to a grid pattern or are winding and higgledy-piggledy. Some have areas of both.

The Greeks used a grid pattern. Here a piece of land is divided into blocks by a criss-cross pattern of roads. The blocks are for houses, squares, markets and so on. This simple and useful plan is still followed today. Most of Manhattan Island in New York is laid out in this way. Many small towns in North America followed the grid pattern until people decided it made these towns look too similar and perhaps boring.

Many Greek and Roman cities were open – not protected by a surrounding wall. After barbarian invaders left them in ruins, city life declined until medieval times. Then many cities were built inside high thick walls. Roads became narrow and winding as more buildings were squeezed in.

You can still see narrow streets like these in many old cities in Europe, North Africa and Asia. When gunpowder and cannons replaced bows and arrows, walls were no longer able to protect the city, but the old pattern of streets inside them was followed when new buildings were added.

▲ Many old cities were originally built like this, with winding streets and higgledy-piggledy blocks inside the outer city walls.

▼ Cities built to a grid pattern have straight roads and regular blocks of buildings.

▲ A United States steel mill in Pittsburgh. Heavy industry like this, with its smoke and fumes, is usually zoned into special areas, away from houses and shops.

▼ The protected Green Belt prevents the city spreading without limit. Inside the city, industry, houses and offices may be zoned into special areas.

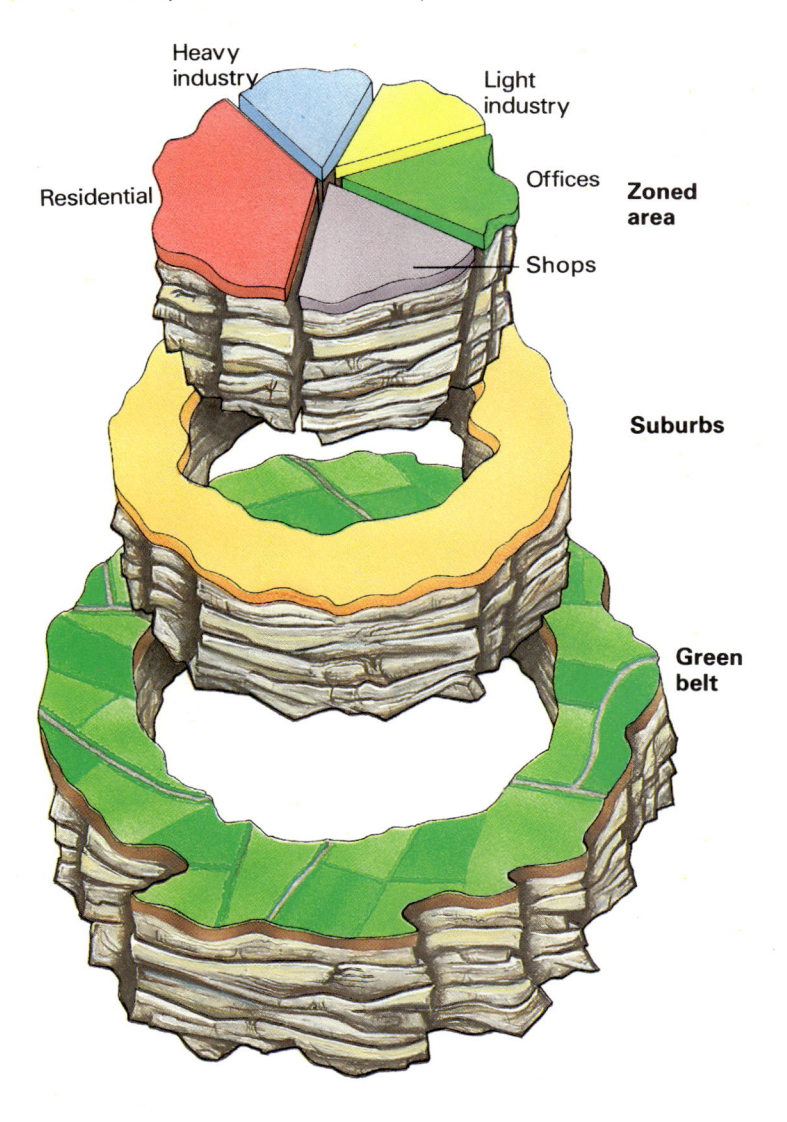

Planning out of chaos

We saw on pages 16 and 17 how the Industrial Revolution took cities by storm. The result of the massive growth in industry and population made planning urgent. Factory owners were allowed to set up industries, mills and workers' houses where they wanted to. The result was a city almost impossible to live in because so much of it was grimy and unhealthy.

It was not until the 20th century that planners had the power to shape the way their cities developed. Zoning and green belts are two ways they control what is built where.

Zoning

Zoning is a form of planning where governments or councils decide what type of building or activity can occur in each area. In one neighbourhood, for example, only houses and local shops may be allowed. Heavy industry is often located in special areas to protect people from its noise and smoke.

Zoning was introduced in New York in 1916 to stop traffic jams and protect the city from being harmed by its own size. The height of buildings was controlled to make sure people on the streets got light.

In the 1960s zoning was attacked. People said it stopped industrial growth by preventing factories being started. It is now less strict.

Green belts

Green belts are rings of countryside outside the city. They are meant to protect the countryside from the outward spread of the city. There is a ring six miles (10 kilometres) wide around Moscow. It is easier to protect than the green belts around London and Tokyo. There is more free land there than in these other two land-hungry cities. Green belts are no longer so popular with planners.

Cities past

◀ The ruins of Teotihuacan in today's Mexico. The Pyramid of the Sun is one of its many religious monuments.

◀ The ancient city of Mohenjo-daro, built more than 4000 years ago in the Indus Valley.

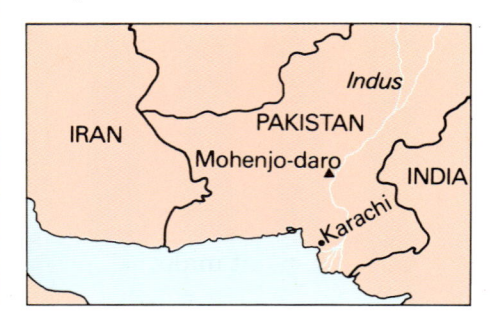

Zoning helps people plan what happens within a city. But, long before modern planning ideas, whole cities were often laid out with a definite idea in mind. On these two pages we shall look at a few to see why they were built the way they were.

Teotihuacan and Peking

Some cities in ancient times were built or planned around places of religious worship. This was true of the first great city in the American continents, Teotihuacan in today's Mexico. Its largest religious monuments, built between AD 100 and 200, were the Pyramid of the Sun, the Pyramid of the Moon and the Temple of Quetzalcoatl.

Around AD 500 the city had between 50 000 and 100 000 inhabitants. Its pyramids and temples drew people to it, but another cause of its growth was its position in good farming land on a main trade route.

The design of 15th century Peking was according to Buddhist beliefs. The layout was meant to help people feel in touch with the laws and rhythms of the Universe.

Mohenjo-daro

Over 4000 years ago Mohenjo-daro in the Indus Valley was one of the most important cities of the ancient Indian civilization. It was carefully laid out and the area for houses was planned on a grid pattern. One of the most important areas was the grain store. Here the city's food was guarded by soldiers. The rulers knew that, if they controlled the food supply, they could rely on the workforce of Mohenjo-daro to be loyal and obedient.

Building for defence

Mohenjo-daro's granary helped to protect the city's rulers from the inhabitants of the city. Other cities were built with walls to protect them, not from their own people, but from outside attack. In medieval times the city wall was one of the causes of city congestion. It prevented the city spreading outwards.

Some cities were built on hills to protect them from attack. Not only did the long climb delay the enemy but the high position was used to spot the oncoming army. The hill towns of Tuscany were protected in this way.

Paris

In Paris in the 1860s Baron Haussmann, ordered by Napoleon III, redesigned the centre of the city. Where there had been narrow winding streets, wide avenues were built. This not only helped make Paris one of the most beautiful cities in the world but also protected the rulers against revolution. Before this, the Paris mob had been able to build barricades in the streets.

Utopia

Some cities were carefully designed but not intended to be built. They were cities of the imagination. Sir Thomas More in England wrote his book *Utopia* in 1516. It described the ideal state, which contained 54 towns and cities. The cities were all alike and were meant to be ideal, perfect settlements where there would be no need for further planning or change.

Social planning

Utopia was never built, but behind every planning scheme there are ideas about how people should live, what makes them happy, and how the society should work.

In the early 1800s Robert Owen turned New Lanark in Scotland into a model industrial village. He gave his workers there more free time, education and better living conditions. He believed that education and the sort of surroundings a person lived in moulded his character.

Another British reformer, Cadbury, built Bournville for the workers of his chocolate factory in the late 19th century, and Lord Lever built Port Sunlight for his soap-factory workers.

These towns were built by factory owners. On the next page we shall see how in 1906 Ebenezer Howard planned the Garden Cities to give people a better life in the countryside away from the grime and misery of the old industrial cities.

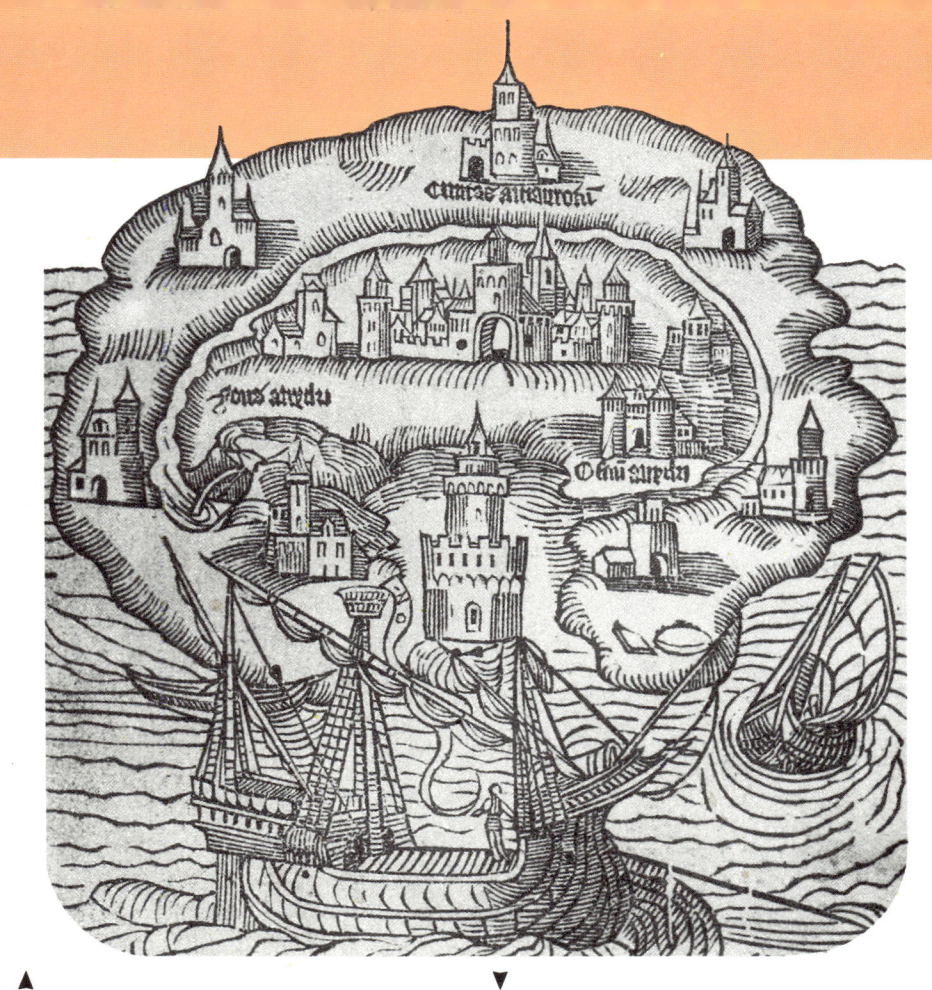

▲ This picture appeared in More's book, *Utopia*. The book described an ideal city and state.

▼ In the 1860s, Napoleon III had a new plan drawn for the centre of Paris. The narrow winding streets were crossed by broad avenues and squares around the Arc de Triomphe, centre bottom of the picture.

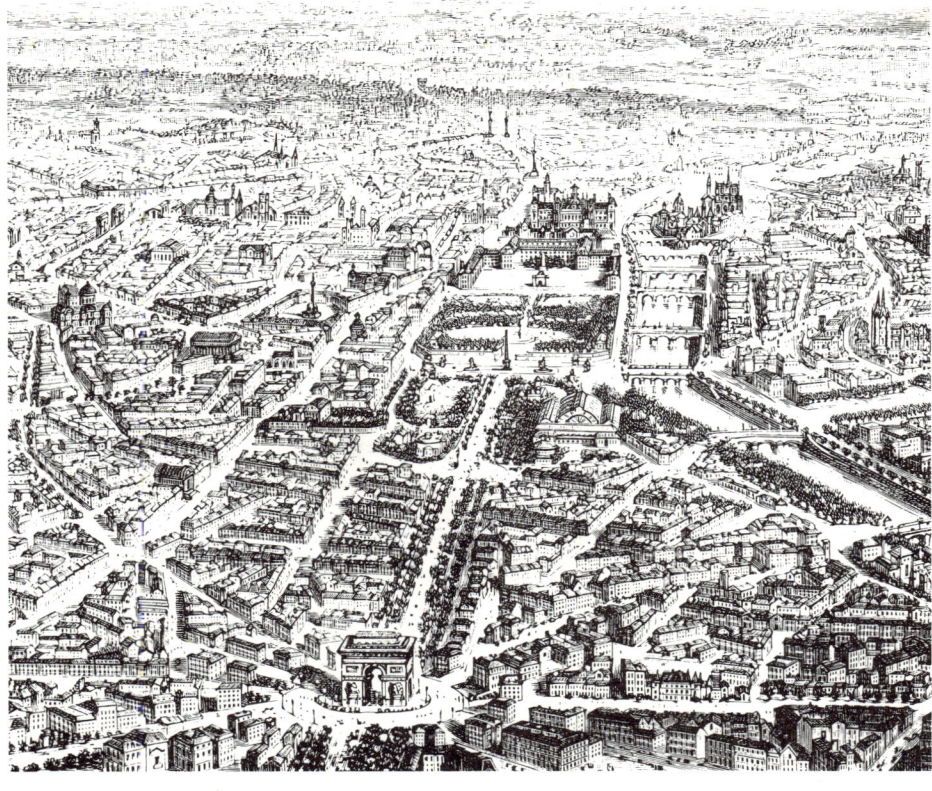

New towns and cities

Most of the new towns and cities built this century have been built with one intention – to move some people and power away from the huge capital cities.

Big cities attract industry, wealth and people. Two problems arise from this. One is that the city gets so big and busy it smothers itself. There are too many traffic jams and urban problems. The other is that, as the big city gets bigger still, it robs smaller areas of their new industry and growth.

Population overspill

One solution to these problems began at the end of the last century when Ebenezer Howard in England formed a plan for Garden Cities. His aim was to rescue people from the grimy main cities. The new cities would be built in the countryside where land was cheap. The beauty and peace would attract people, but Garden Cities would also offer all the advantages of town life.

Letchworth was the first of the Garden Cities to be built. They have all become successful in their own right.

New Towns were designed with the clearer aim of helping the main city by draining off extra people, many of whom may still travel to the main city to work. These are called satellite towns. Let us see how they have been used to help Paris cope with its problems.

Paris eats France

In 1960 Paris was so huge the rest of France looked like its backyard. There were almost eight million people in and around it. Only two cities elsewhere in France had more than half a million people. The danger was that Paris would attract more and more activity. As a result other towns and regions would not grow.

To discourage industry in Paris the Government imposed heavy taxes. To prevent people just moving to the outskirts of the city, five industrial and

▲ Milton Keynes is about 46 miles (74 kilometres) from London. This Garden City was planned with many open spaces to give people the best of living in the countryside and the city.

▼ Tapiola is a Garden City built near Helsinki in Finland. These two views show how the architects have paid as much attention to essential shopping centres as they have to the lush, green residential areas.

▲ These Space-Age buildings are in Brasilia, South America. They look exciting but do not help to make the city lively or friendly.

▼ Tokyo and Yokohama are really one place. They are protected by a Green Belt. Tokyo has spread beyond the Green Belt and many satellite towns have been built within 70 miles (130 kilometres) of the two cities.

housing areas were planned in the basin of the River Seine near Paris. Express trains were laid on to take people into Paris. In addition several old towns were given special help by the State so that they could grow too.

Other New Towns
Plans to build New Towns were set in motion in Britain in 1946. By the 1980s about two million people lived in them. London has ten New Towns around it.

In Sweden New Towns have been built around Stockholm. Most of the land is owned by the State and most of the services are provided by Stockholm. In Finland a satellite town called Tapiola has been built near Helsinki, not with government money, but with money from private companies.

Not all New Towns work well. In Britain they have drawn too many skilled people from the main cities and left behind too many of the unemployed. They can be boring and socially dead places. Cumbernauld in Scotland has a high rate of crime, unemployment and alcoholism.

New capitals of government
New cities are not always built to drain big city overspill. Canberra in Australia and Washington DC in America were built as capitals of government. They were also meant to stand as a sign of national pride.

Brasilia in Brazil was built to be an impressive city that would show the world how modern and full of energy the country was. It was designed to open up an area of Brazil that had been neglected by business and industry. An enormous amount of money was spent flying building materials to the site. Strangely, Brasilia is not a great social success. There is a lack of the bustle and liveliness that you find in most cities. The liveliest areas, in fact, are the shanty towns that have grown up, unplanned, outside it.

Futuristic schemes

◀ One architect's fantasy – a city on different floors of a giant skyscraper.

To build a real city you need bricks, concrete, machines and workmen. Once it is finished you want it to work well so you have not wasted your money and time. But none of this need worry you when you dream of a perfect city. Now you can close your eyes and imagine – what? Cities built inside a giant metal shell which can be moved around on wheels? A city with one building, but a building 10 miles (16 kilometres) high? What would your dream city look like?

Many architects have asked themselves that question and come up with an answer. Some have become so interested in their dream cities they have tried to build them. This takes more than dreams and money. The architect has to work out all the building details so that his city stands up to wind, heat, cold and rain, and other stresses and strains.

Arcosanti
An architect called Paolo Soleri took his plans into the desert in America and started to build. Gifted with the ability to make others enthusiastic, Soleri found people willing to pay him to work on his project. Inside the city you will live his dream, because the design is his alone. Other cities are the product of many architects.

Most dream cities are never built. But it is very important for architects and planners to have futuristic dreams. Some of the ideas they may come up with could be useful, rather than just weird. Take the idea of Ocean City, for example.

◀ People pay for the chance of working at Arcosanti, an architect's dream city in the Arizona desert.

◀ Could a bubble like this be built over mid-town Manhattan in New York and other cities to create a special climate there?

Ocean City

Japan is a small country with a huge population. Only 18 per cent of its land can be used as living space because two thirds is mountainous. So where can new cities go? There is a plan to build a city in the sea.

The Ocean City scheme could be as expensive as the city in space project (see pages 56 and 57). Four decks would be built on stilts in the sea. The top deck would have houses for two million people, as well as shops and parks. On other decks would be factories, sewage systems and other services.

This city could be constructed and would help to solve Japan's shortage of space. But is it worth the money and do people now or beyond AD 2000 want to live in artificial cities?

▼ The Japanese plan to build Ocean City to house up to 2 million of their population.

Preserving the past

Building whole new cities may be exciting, but it is vastly expensive. Many people feel that the best way forward is to preserve and improve the buildings we already have. In the past only important buildings were saved when they were no longer strictly needed. These included old government buildings, churches and grand mansions. Today we try to save more than this, and, in the future, plans to tear down even old run-down houses will be looked at very closely.

One reason is that tearing down houses to build new ones is expensive. In London plans to tear down many areas ran into trouble when councils found they did not have enough money for the rebuilding. Instead, they now try to repair and restore the old houses. This is cheaper and keeps alive a link with the past. Could this become a common policy all over the world in 2000?

Venice

Buildings of historic and artistic interest have always been protected. People do not want to see palaces, museums and art galleries torn down by bulldozers. But there are other threats to beautiful old cities.

Venice in Italy has 400 buildings listed as of high artistic interest, but the whole city is being damaged by a rise in sea level. Ground on the mainland which soaked up water was drained so factories could be placed there. A channel was dug to allow bigger ships to dock in the city. Both of these caused the sea level to rise, and as the water rises the ground is slowly sinking. In 1966 unusual tides and winds flooded the city causing damage in two days that would otherwise have taken fifty years.

At first the Italian government did not take the fight to save Venice seriously enough. But now much more money has been spent. Beyond the year 2000, though, we may still be watching this great city sink into the sea as its foundations weaken.

Warsaw

Preserving a city sometimes means more than just not pulling it down. Hundreds of towns and cities in Europe were shattered during World War 2. Warsaw in Poland was one of these. Hitler wanted it completely destroyed – nothing left standing and no one alive. By the end of the war, 84 per cent of the city was gone. Some people wanted to abandon it, but instead it was rebuilt. Some areas were made to look exactly as they did before. Pieces of the old buildings were saved from the wreckage and used on the new.

Cuzco

Cuzco in Peru was the centre of the Inca empire. Today buildings and walls of the Incas are preserved. Another layer in the city's history can be seen in the Spanish colonial buildings which remain. In addition, the city is a busy place in the present and the centre of a region of small towns and villages high up on the slopes of the Andes.

The Incas built Cuzco around AD 1100 and it became the centre of the four provinces of their empire. The ruler controlled an area from today's Equador to Argentina. The Inca civilization has died out and its remains in cities like Cuzco and Machu Picchu in Peru are extremely valuable. To lose them would be to lose contact with an important piece of history.

Conservation areas

Modern civilization also needs to be preserved. There is often a battle between conservation societies and governments about what to save and what to sacrifice. Business puts its weight behind tearing down the old to make way for the new. If people did not fight this, some areas preserved today would not exist.

One way of protecting present buildings is used in Britain where conservation areas are declared. Here no one may alter their house in a way which changes the character of the neighbourhood. They often have to get permission for even small changes. This is the way many people want cities to be protected as the year 2000 comes closer. Will it happen?

This square in Warsaw was rebuilt just as it was before bombs flattened the city in World War 2. The old city rose again from the rubble and ash.

Chimney rebuilt

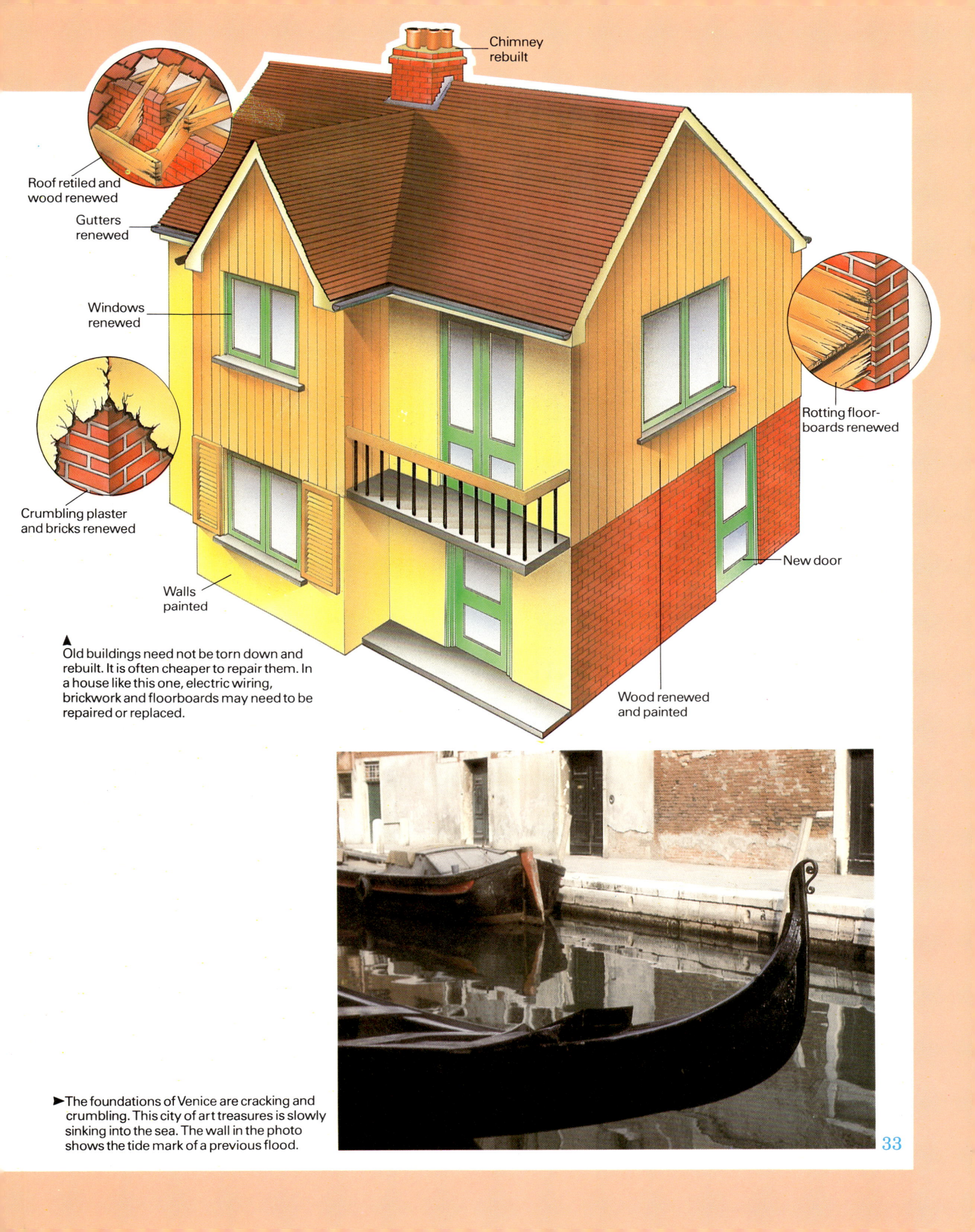

Roof retiled and wood renewed

Gutters renewed

Windows renewed

Crumbling plaster and bricks renewed

Walls painted

Rotting floorboards renewed

New door

Wood renewed and painted

▲ Old buildings need not be torn down and rebuilt. It is often cheaper to repair them. In a house like this one, electric wiring, brickwork and floorboards may need to be repaired or replaced.

►The foundations of Venice are cracking and crumbling. This city of art treasures is slowly sinking into the sea. The wall in the photo shows the tide mark of a previous flood.

33

CHAPTER 4
Building the city

City planners and architects try to solve urban problems. They want to improve housing and create areas where business and factories will succeed.

Take the common problem of shortage of land in cities. One solution has been to build skyscrapers, and this has affected the look of many big cities, particularly in America. People have predicted even more skyscrapers for the year 2000. Further than that, there may be whole cities in the sky (see pages 30 and 31). In this chapter we shall look at building in the city – highrise, lowrise, even underground building.

The first skyscrapers
Some historians have guessed that the first skyscrapers were apartment buildings in Ancient Rome. This might be true, but the real beginnings of the modern skyscraper were apartment towers built in Manhattan, New York, in the mid 1900s. Land was so expensive people wanted to use as little as possible to house as many people as possible. Americans were used to open spaces and, at first, did not like living one on top of the other in these new apartments.

New Yorkers finally accepted life in apartments when they realized they were not very different from hotels. The many-storeyed apartments built in Paris along the city's beautiful avenues also helped to persuade Americans to give up the one-family-one-house idea. Today many people enjoy living in comfortable highrise apartments.

Tower blocks
Apartments of 19th century New York were very different from the many tall tower blocks built particularly in the 1960s for less well-off people. At the time these were thought to be a brilliant answer to the need for more space. The skyscrapers would be a good distance from each other and would be set in gardens for people to look down on or stroll in.

The scheme did not work because tenants felt cut off from the world outside and trapped in small boxes in the sky. The sense of living in a community of neighbours was destroyed. The towers became easy places for mugging and other crimes. Because tenants weren't proud to live in them, the buildings became filthy and broken-down and covered in graffiti. Many have had to be pulled down.

Highrise living looked good at the design stage, but was a social failure. Some cities made the problem worse by dumping problem families or the very poor or unemployed in the least popular blocks. Some of these were then wrecked and abandoned by their tenants.

Skyscraper offices are much more successful. The first was the ten-storey Home Insurance Company building put up in Chicago in 1884.

▲ Highrise building in Hong Kong. Hong Kong has to fit very many people into a small space, so houses, shops and offices have to be built high.

Building a skyscraper
Skyscrapers have a steel frame around which the walls are built. This metal skeleton is strong enough to stay upright in gales and milder earthquakes. At first fire was a great threat. The heat would have melted the frame and caused the whole building to collapse. Then fireproofing to protect the frame was invented.

Another vital invention was the lift or elevator. No one wants to walk six or ten floors to work, much less fifty or a hundred! Plumbing, heating, cooling and lighting systems also had to be especially designed for skyscrapers. The first complete mechanical system of cooling and ventilation was used in Buffalo in the United States in 1904.

By the year 2000 we may be able to erect a building a kilometre (0.6 miles) high. But will we want to? Skyscrapers make people feel they are like ants living and working among giant metal and glass anthills.

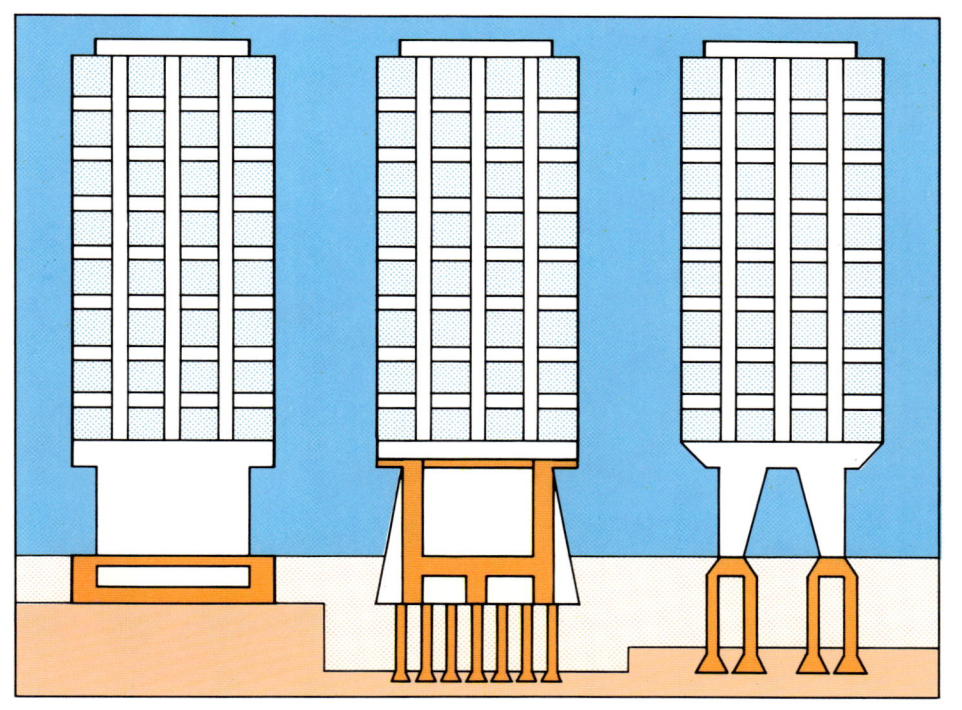

▲ These diagrams show three different ways of building skyscrapers. The type of foundation used depends on the condition of the ground on which they are built.

▼ As problems of damp, noise and loneliness increased, people refused to live in some highrise blocks. These council flats in London had to be blown up.

World's highest buildings

Tallest structure:
Warsaw Radio mast   2120.6 ft
    (646.4 metres)

Tallest office buildings:
Sears Tower, Chicago   1559 ft
    (475.2 metres)
World Trade Center,   1353 ft
    New York   (412.4 metres)

Tallest apartment block:
Lake Point Towers,   645 ft
    Chicago   (196.6 metres)

Tallest hotel:
Peachtree Center Plaza,   723 ft
    Atlanta   (220.4 metres)

Building low

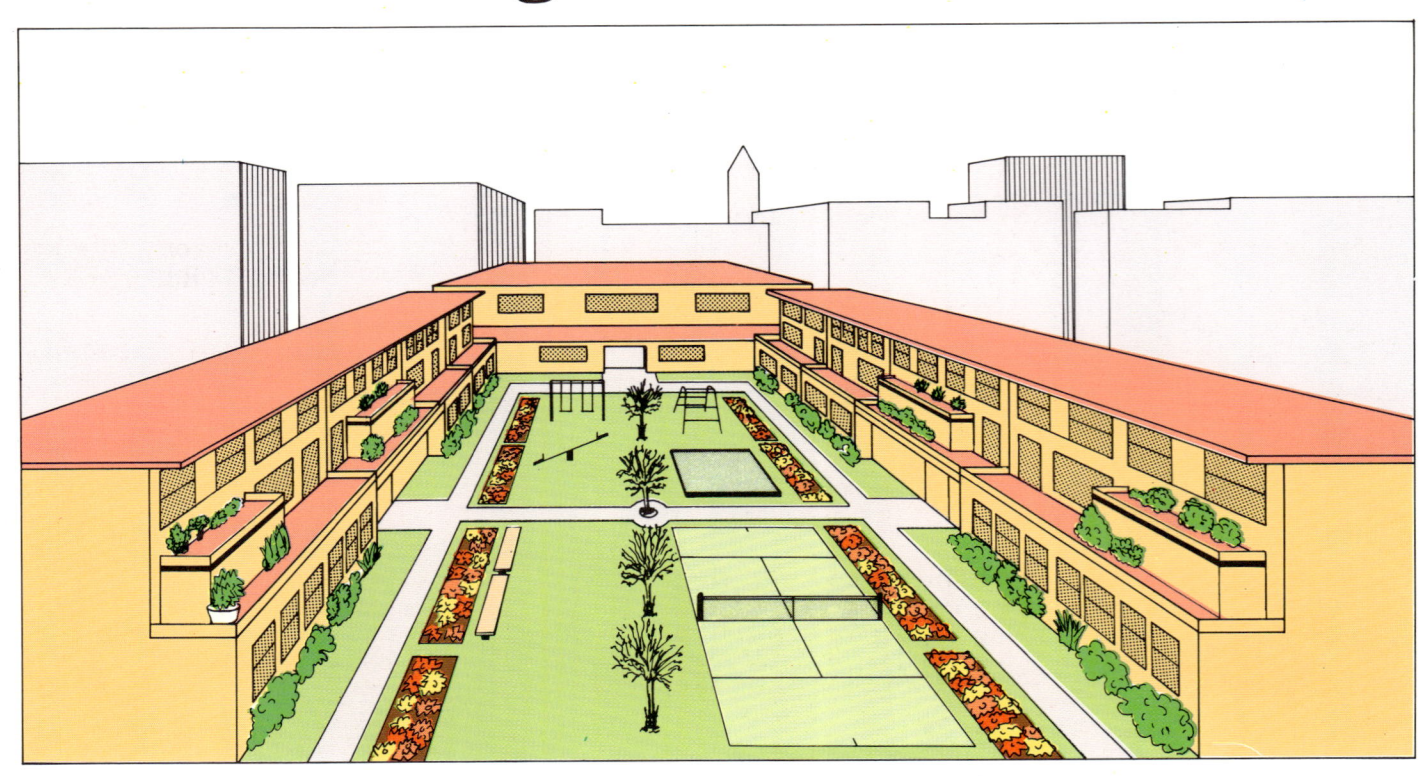

A low-level scheme may house many people and provide a safe and friendly place in which to live.

Skyscrapers are not the only possible answer to the land shortage question. As we saw on the last page piling homes on top of each other inside a concrete tube does not work. People living in them feel isolated. Other answers have to be found.

High-density, lowrise
The lowrise housing estate is the solution used today. It has been much more successful. Apartments are in buildings a few storeys high at most. These are arranged around an open space in the centre of the estate – a square, play area or garden. Looking out of the window parents can keep an eye on children playing. Separated from the public street by buildings, the children are safe from traffic.

The windows on the other side of the estate look out on to the street outside. This keeps tenants in touch with the neighbourhood. Often there is an open corridor on this side. The front doors to the flats lead off it. Big estates may cover many city blocks and have services inside them, such as play schools or shopping centres. But no matter how big they are, their height is kept down and the surroundings are more friendly and personal. This solution fits the same number of people into the same area as the old highrise did.

Low-density, lowrise
Because the need for land is not so urgent outside the city centre, suburbs contain fewer people to each acre. Houses can afford to be low, perhaps no more than two storeys high. There are gardens and parks and people live more privately.

While skyscrapers tend to look the same, houses do not. Houses in different parts of the world look more traditional. Builders use materials available locally and this helps style the houses. In New England on the American east coast clapboard houses are built using a lot of local wood for the walls.

In hot countries walls may be thick to keep the houses cooler in summer. In small poorer settlements in Greece, many people live in unfinished houses. When they can afford to, they build a bit more onto the house.

One of the most common building materials is mud. Along with timber, thatch, stone, lime, bitumen and sometimes dung, mud is used widely in the Third World. It is combined with other cheap materials to make it stronger.

Architects versus local styles
In the developed world houses are designed by architects. In the Third World you may build the house yourself. But this does not make the houses there less attractive or strong. People in Africa and India decorate the outside walls by painting brilliant designs on them. Mud-roofed houses in Iran look like space-age settlements. Shopping centres in Egypt mix styles which suggest the future with those that awaken thoughts about settlements in the distant past. Houses like these have been built for centuries and will

▲
The sprawling lowrise suburbs of Perth, Western Australia.

▶ Cities which are short of space may decide to build under the ground. This plan provides shops, restaurants and trains, all below street level.

continue to be built far into the next century.

Money or the lack of it affects lowrise housing all over the world. In rural Africa a man must spend ten days' wages to buy one bag of cement. In Europe one day's earnings of a poor person would buy ten bags.

Building down
People have thought of finding more building space underground. There are other reasons for building down. In Montreal, for example, shopping centres built below ground level are easier to heat during the freezing Canadian winter. In China some factories have been built underground to protect them from a nuclear war.

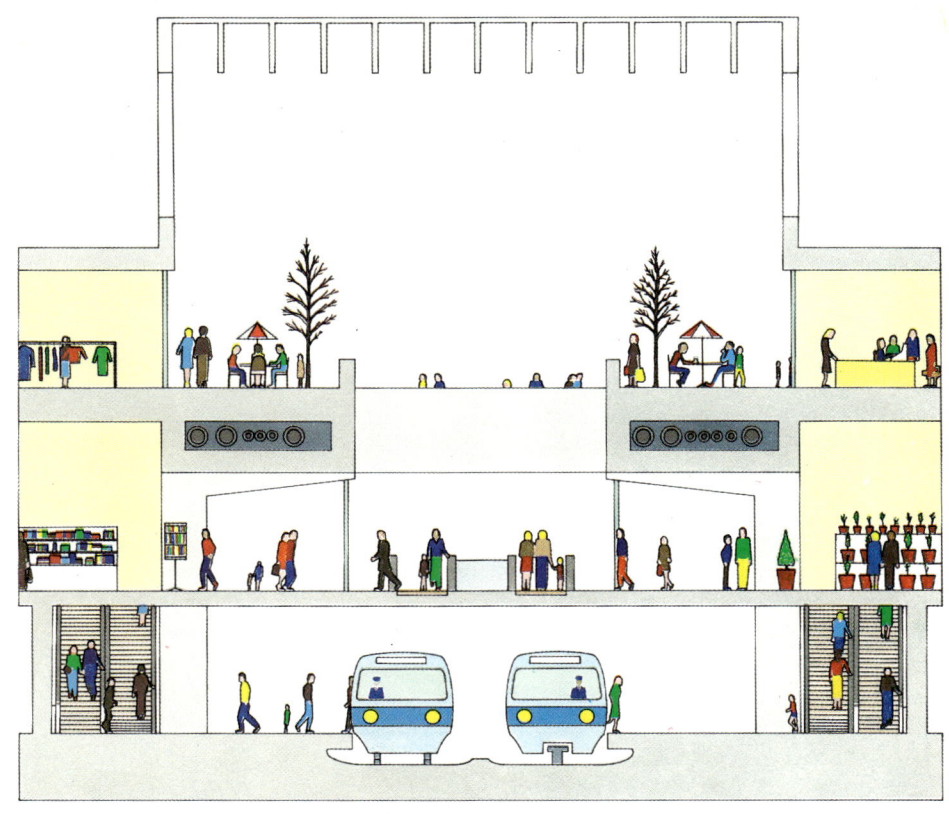

Tomorrow's home

Today's houses leak heat. It gets out through ill-fitting windows and doors, thin walls, window panes, roofs or down waste pipes. And what is used is used only once. With the world's resources of fossil fuels running low, stopping the daily waste is an urgent matter. And, with homes using a quarter or more of all the rich nations' energy, it is vital that houses become heat traps not heat sieves. Existing houses can be made more efficient and new houses can be specially designed to hold heat in and re-use it time and again.

Efficient heat

By wrapping special material around hot water tanks the heat is sealed in. A whole attic can be lined with material to act as a barrier to heat created in the rooms below. We can seal the cracks at the edges of windows in winter to exclude draughts.

We can go further and inject a type of foam into hollow walls and fit an extra pane of glass over the windows. This can save 40 or 50 per cent of the energy created inside the house.

Heat-trap house

An energy conservation house built specially for that purpose uses natural heat whenever possible. The sun heats water tanks in the roof and warms the air in a greenhouse. This air is conducted to other rooms. The house is built on a stone slab which heats up during the day and releases the heat into the house at night. Trees shield the dwelling from the wind. Solar panels in the roof can absorb heat from the sun and use it to heat water or the house.

No heat is lost from this kind of house, and so ventilation has to be installed with special care. Opening a window to get fresh air would allow too much heat to escape. In future many more ventilation systems will use the hot stuffy air inside to heat the

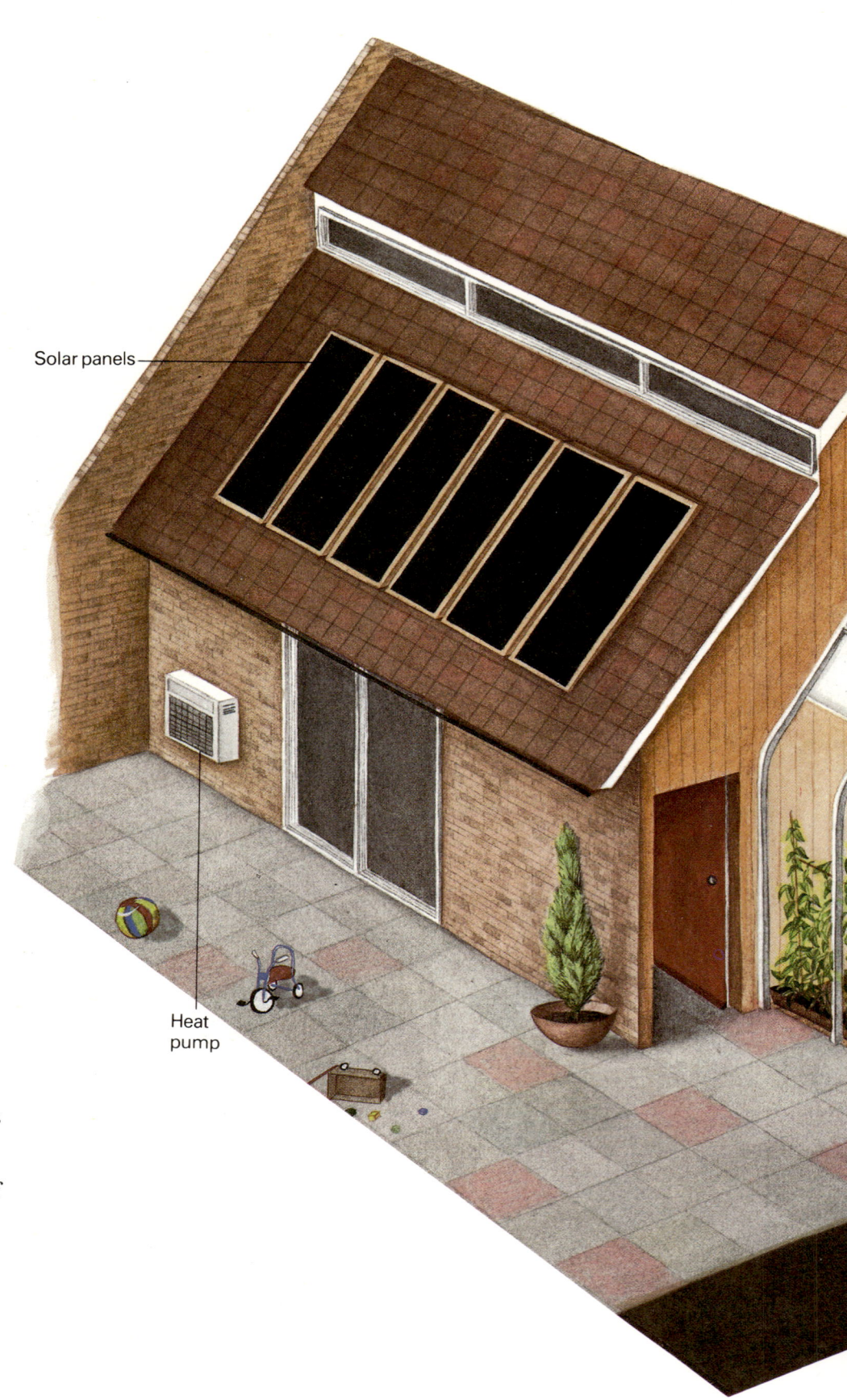

Solar panels

Heat pump

The heat-trap house captures the warmth of the sun. Heat inside the house cannot escape and is used to the maximum.

Bank and trees to provide shelter on side of house away from sun

Floor and rock bed absorb heat during the day and release it at night

cool fresh air coming in. Only when the heat has been transferred will the used-up air be expelled.

It may even be possible to transfer heat from bathwater to some other use before it drains away. Excrement could be made into fuel and burned to create more energy, and a windmill outside could trap the energy of the wind.

Specially designed low-energy houses have to face the sun and should be built into a bank. This is not always possible in a city and there will probably be few heat-trap houses in the year 2000. Nevertheless some of their ideas will be used in our homes.

New equipment
The search for energy conservation has produced some important devices which will be used in ordinary homes as well as in special heat-trap houses.

One is a heat-pump which draws heat from the air or ground outside and uses it to heat the house. The heat-pump basically up-grades, that is makes hotter, the air from the outside to heat the house inside.

Another device is the photovoltaic cell which can be fixed to a roof or wall. It converts sunlight into electricity which can be used to heat water in a tank or to help run household appliances. These new devices will soon be available at local shops.

Government action
The main emphasis will be on making existing homes better. Pressure will be put on governments to help by advancing money for conservation materials and equipment. The West German Government has announced a two-billion dollar grant to private houses for insulation, heat pumps and solar technology.

Inside the home

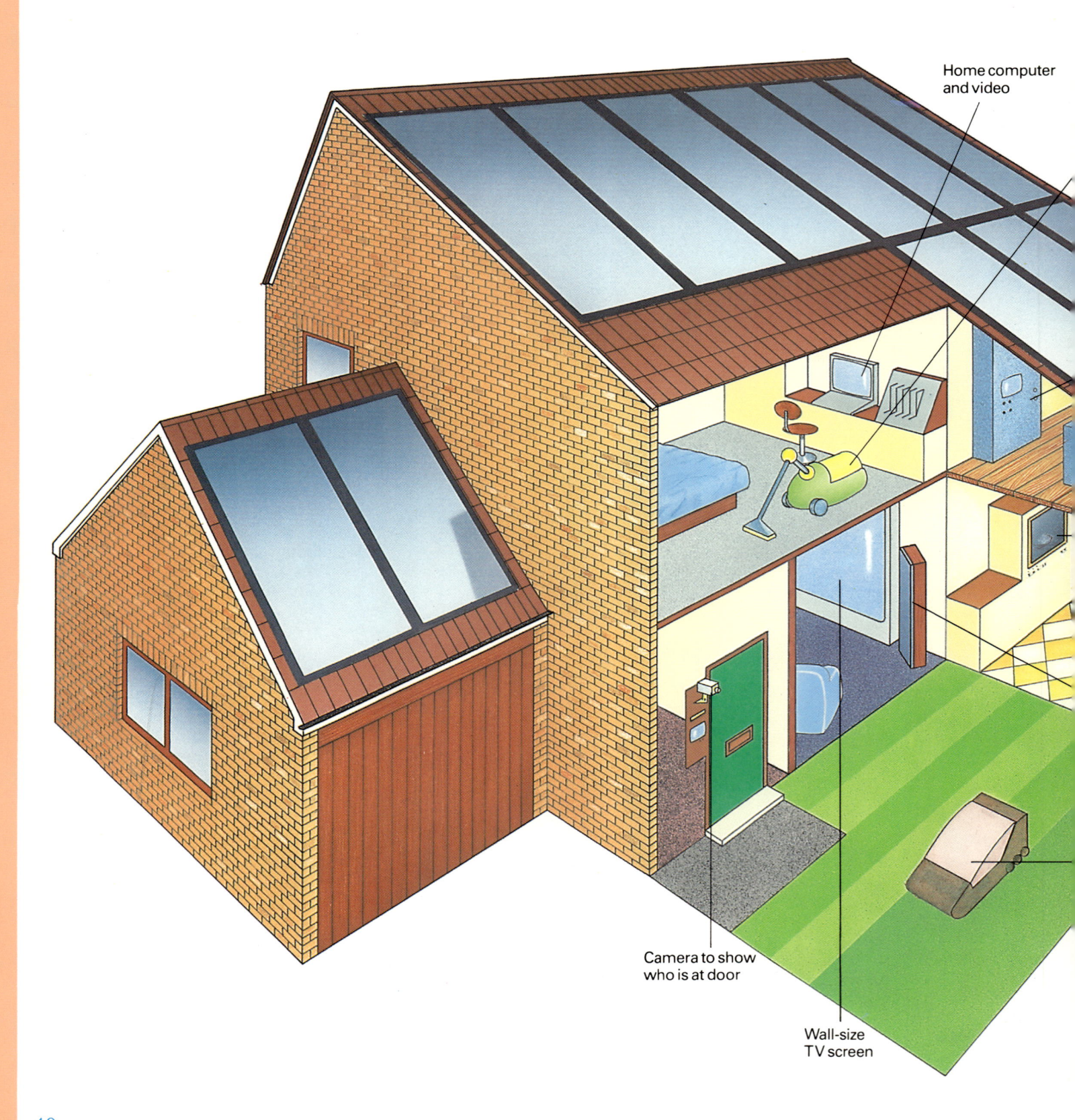

Home computer and video

Camera to show who is at door

Wall-size TV screen

Energy and space will be used more efficiently in the up-to-date house of the future. Rooms will be used for a range of different activities. There will be a central computer to control the kitchen, the sitting room and probably the bedroom and bathroom too.

Computers use very little electricity but can operate complicated machines. They can, for example, make a central heating system work more efficiently. We waste electricity in the home today because it is up to us to control the supply. So we leave kettles to boil and turn stoves up too high. The heating system may warm rooms that are not used much along with ones that are. The hot-water tank may be kept going all day although no one is planning a bath. In future, computers and microprocessors will automatically control the creation of heat so that only the exactly right amount is used.

A microprocessor's 'brain' consists of silicon chips. With silicon chips, machines can be programmed in such detail that they can be left alone to get on with jobs like cooking or house-cleaning.

The kitchen
Today, most washing machines can be pre-set to fill with water, wash and spin dry before turning themselves off. Cookers, too, can go through complicated routines without further attention after being turned on. In the near future it may even be possible to phone the cooker from the office and instruct it to get to work. The right signals from the human voice will turn it on.

Today's kitchen gadgets will perform better in the future, and more people will have them. Dishwashers will handle all the washing up including pots and pans. Most kitchens will probably have a microwave oven. Snacks such as hamburgers will be cooked in a few minutes, and food taken straight from the freezer will be thawed and cooked in a matter of minutes.

The living room
Television and video screens will have more uses than today. Visitors at the front door will appear on a screen so you can decide whether you want to let them in.

A computer in the home will link you to your bank account and to accounts in local shops and supermarkets. You will be able to sit at home, punch out on a keyboard what food you want to order from the local supermarket, and instruct your bank account to pay for it. Details and prices of goods in local shops will be available through a television information system.

You will also be able to get a mass of other information by linking into a central computer. It may be possible to link several people in different parts of the world and talk to them on screen, almost as though they were in the same room as you.

The bathroom
People have guessed that in future you will stand in a tub and nozzles will automatically spray you with jets of warm water. You will see an image of your body on a screen and be able to check how the modern washing method is getting on. But the machine will sense when you are clean and turn itself off. This will not appeal to people who like to take long leisurely baths.

How much will change?
Changes like these will all eventually be possible. Two facts are important though. One is that super-modern appliances will be expensive so that only rich people will be able at first to live in the total electronic house.

The other is that new electronic inventions sound weird and fantastic, but may not actually be so. For example, people talk about robots making your morning tea, but machines like these already exist. They are fun, but they have not made getting up in the morning very different or much easier.

Labels: Robot vacuum cleaner; Solar panels; Computer to control central heating; Microwave oven; Laser hot plates; Giant hi-fi speaker; Robot lawn mower

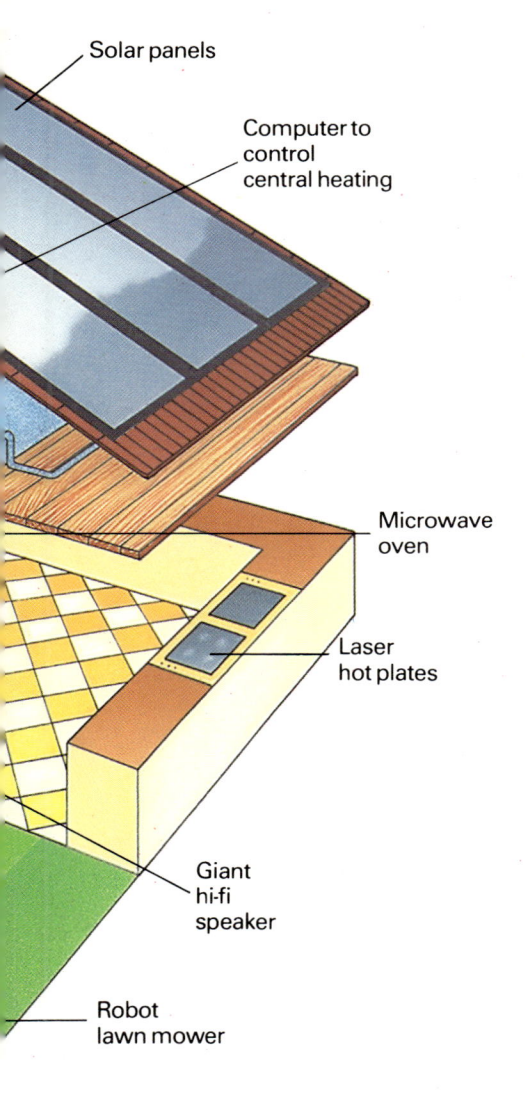

The inside of tomorrow's home may look very different from today's. Microcomputers will be responsible for many of the changes.

CHAPTER 5
Living in the city

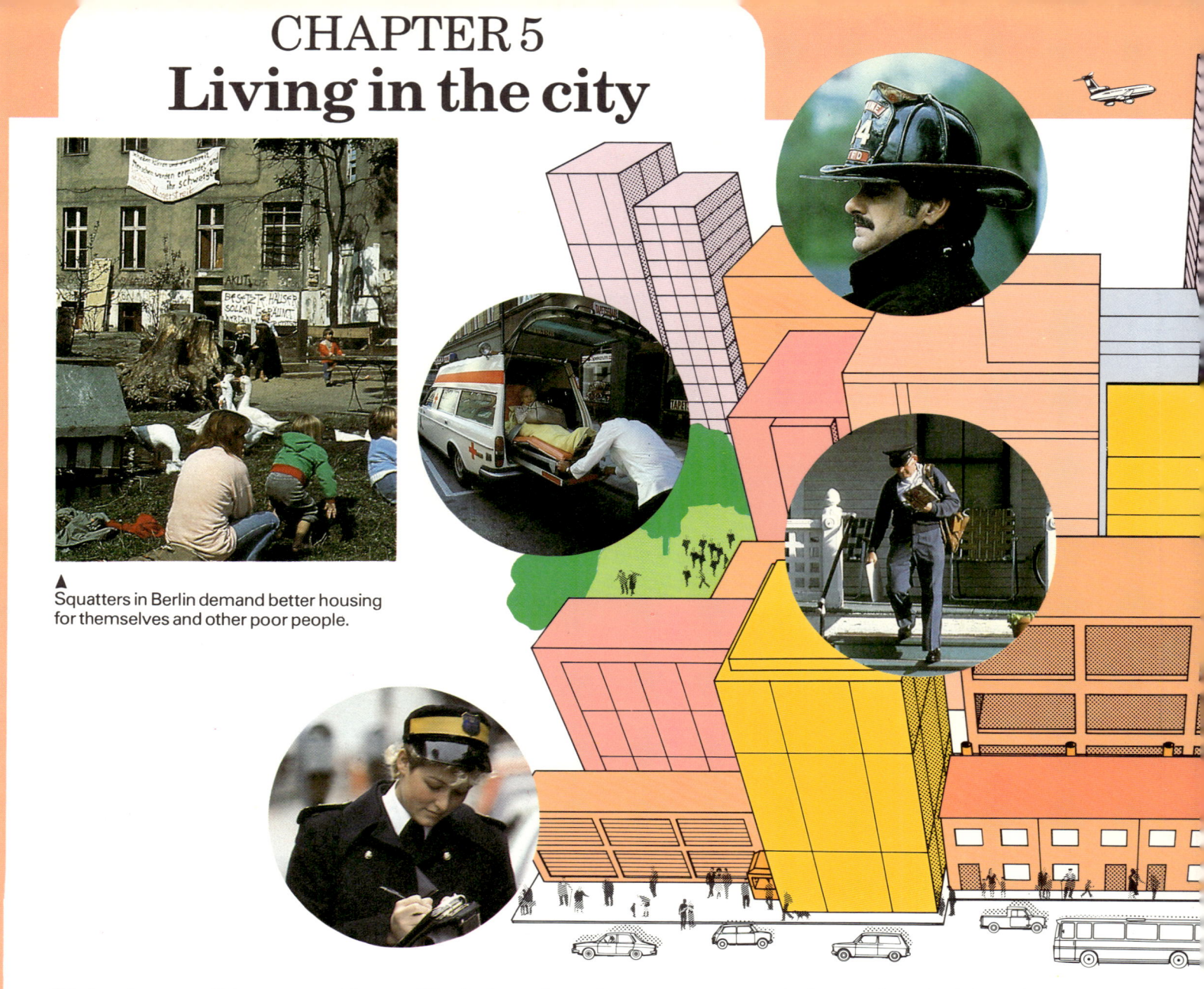

Squatters in Berlin demand better housing for themselves and other poor people.

Living in a small town or on the land we may spend our time in many different ways. But once we move to a big city our choices are multiplied. And there are not only very many different things we may do each day, there are also different ways in which we can live. Variety is what cities are famous for.

In a city we may live in a house, a hotel, an apartment, or a room. We may live in one of many different parts of town: an old area near the centre where there is life on the streets, say, or a quiet suburban neighbourhood. On top of a residential skyscraper we may look down over miles and miles of concrete dotted with parks and perhaps divided by a river.

Varieties of work
In small towns the types of work we may do are limited. In cities there are many more ways of making a living. The head offices of big companies are in main cities. National newspapers, television, advertising, insurance and banking are usually centred in big cities. There are often more opportunities for technical workers, builders, secretaries and local government workers. City hospitals need a larger staff and the poorest areas of cities, where there are social problems, need social workers.

We have seen how people in the Third World try to escape from grinding rural poverty to the cities. If they do not find industrial work there, they seize whatever opportunities they can find, from washing cars to selling nuts, from shining shoes to weighing people on a set of scales in the middle of the teeming pavements.

A hard life
All this may make living in cities sound easy and wonderful. City life in fact is often hard. There is much competition and people have to work hard and struggle. Not everyone can live in a luxury apartment with beautiful views and a built-in sauna.

What you can do in a city often depends on how much money you have. Someone living in an apartment with damp walls and poor heating in winter may have a

▲ Florida is a playground for rich people. Being rich or poor can make a difference to how you feel about city life.

▲ Cities provide a great variety of jobs. In the future more of these jobs will be like those shown here – policeman, traffic warden, bill sticker, refuse collector, ambulance driver, fireman and postman – jobs in service industries, some of them paid for by the city corporation.

different story of city life than someone who can afford to eat in good restaurants.

As an answer to housing problems some people have tried squatting. They have moved into houses that have been left vacant by councils and owners. They claim that, because the houses were not lived in for many years, they have a right to live there free. Squatting, which is similar to the illegal occupation of land in shanty towns, is strictly outlawed in some countries. But there was a great deal of squatting in European cities in the 1970s and there still is in many parts of Amsterdam and London.

City characteristics
As we shall see on pages 52 and 53 there is a danger that cities will grow more alike. Despite that, many cities today, particularly older ones, have a character of their own. Rome, Paris, London, New York, Vienna, Rio de Janiero, Istanbul are just a few of the world's famous cities where visitors arrive in thousands to experience the special character of the city.

Paris is a grand city with beautiful avenues and squares. It is also charming with many areas where narrow old streets twist and turn. In Rome the ruins of the ancient classical city are surrounded by the bustle of the crowded 20th century city.

Millions of people flock to London to see its superb palaces, parks, art galleries and fashionable houses. Millions too visit Istanbul, which could hardly be more different from London. Here the old part of the city is jammed with crowds and traffic, bakers and bootmakers, work and trade. Traders sell sherbet from huge containers on their backs and men sit in cafés drinking Turkish tea and renting huge hookahs – pipes where the tobacco smoke is drawn through a pot of cooling water.

43

Working in the city

◀ Japanese commuters pour out of the station on their way to work. As computers take over more and more jobs and companies move out of the city centre, will such a sight become a thing of the past?

Great changes are taking place in our cities. They are largely the result of changes in the work that city dwellers do.

At one time the cities of the West were the world centres of manufacture. They became rich by producing goods such as steel, textiles, railway engines. Many city people worked in factories and offices, but new technology is changing all this. Jobs which were done by people can now be done by computers, or by machines which are controlled by computers. For example, by the year 2000 more and more trains will have no drivers, but be operated by computer 'brains'.

It is now possible to make smaller computers and ones which can do more complicated things. On pages 40 and 41 we saw how microelectronics will make household chores easier and more efficient. In factories and offices computers will be able to do more and more jobs. Already robots assemble cars faster and more reliably than people.

By operating a simple keyboard, like a typewriter, newspaper journalists can now have their stories set straight onto film ready to be printed. Before, a worker called a compositor had to set the journalist's story with metal letters before it could be printed.

In the next twenty years, advances in electronics will bring great changes in the way we work. Large cities have always been storehouses of information. But now a businessman in a small town can use a computer linked to a large central information system to get the latest prices or news in seconds. Will this lead to companies leaving big cities because there is no reason for them to be there? This is already happening in some parts of Europe and the US.

People could even work from home, using a computer linked to the telephone system to communicate with their clients and colleagues, possibly on the other side of the world. People who prefer to work with other people around them may find an office near their home where they can have company and can share the use and cost of expensive electronic equipment.

Service industries
Manufacturing industries in the richer countries now employ fewer people than before. But there has been an increase in industries which offer a service, like banking or insurance. By 1980, 60 per cent of Canadian workers were employed in services, and only 29 per cent in industries which manufactured goods for sale.

In the richer countries of the world the shift from industry to services has brought serious problems. When factory buildings lie idle, large areas of the city decay. Business has to be encouraged to move there.

Unemployment
In the 1980s unemployment became a major problem in the West for the first time in fifty years. By 1984 the United Kingdom, with a total population of over 55 million, had over 3·5 million people without jobs.

▶ Computer rooms similar to this one are already found in many firms. By the year 2000, few large-scale businesses will survive without one.

Unemployment affects certain sections of society more harshly than others – the young and unqualified for instance.

Some countries run schemes to train people in the skills needed by the new technologies. These new ways of working, however, do not provide many jobs. Rather than paying people unemployment pay, some governments are providing money for large projects, such as modernizing the railways and repairing old houses. These projects can employ many people. Some governments have been more successful than others in tackling the problem, but it will not go away altogether.

People need to work, not just for money, but for a feeling of pride. By the year 2000, however, richer countries can expect to see a shorter working week, earlier retirement, and more job sharing. At the same time people will be healthier and live longer.

We must ensure that time spent not working is not therefore wasted. Pages 50 and 51 looks at some of the ways people can enjoy leisure time in the city. Videos may also provide hours of cheap entertainment as well as a chance for people to learn new craft skills and even to study for a degree.

▶ As nations become more industrialized, fewer people work in agriculture, more people work in manufacturing industries and, eventually, most people work in service industries.

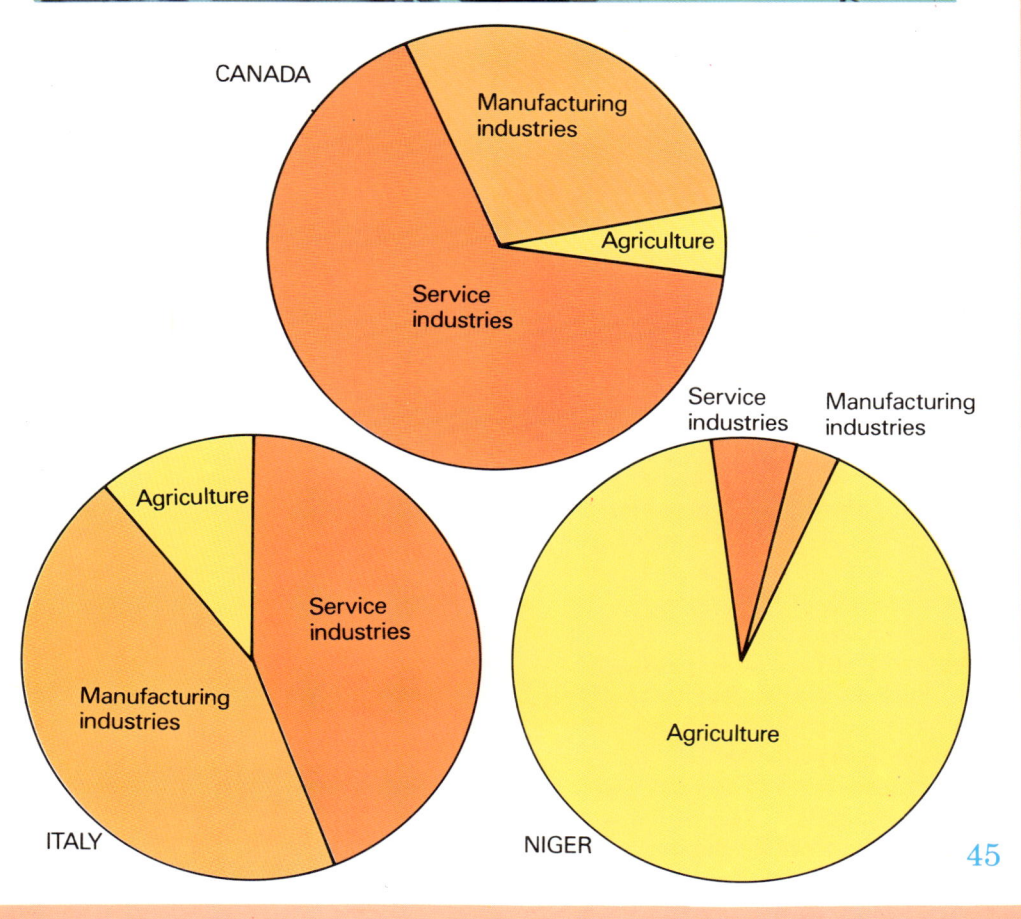

On the road

The invention of the internal combustion engine in the last century gave people complete freedom of movement for the first time – but at a cost.

Motor cars pollute the air. Gasoline (petrol) may contain unhealthy amounts of lead and exhaust fumes produce smog which shrouds cities like Mexico City or like Los Angeles, on the sunny west coast of the United States. Traffic jams in Lagos, Nigeria, are so bad they have encouraged plans to build a brand new capital city at Abuja. All over the world, flyovers, ring roads and urban expressways carve their way through cities, dividing local communities and destroying buildings.

By the 1980s steps were being taken to save cities from the car. Some countries brought in laws to control how much lead can be added to gasoline (petrol). Cars have been banned from some central city areas. People use public transport and are allowed to walk in the car-free streets.

In the 1970s people began to realize that, since the world's stocks of oil are limited, oil will become more and more expensive. Engineers are now designing cars which use less fuel, or fuel made from plants, and electric cars which are powered by batteries.

The future
The cars of the future must be small and efficient – not the 'gas-guzzlers' popular for so many years in the United States. Great improvements in fuel consumption are already being made.

The ECV3 (Energy Conservation Vehicle) is an experimental model produced by British Leyland. In city traffic it uses a gallon of fuel every 49 miles (a litre every 17 kilometres). On the motorway, at a steady speed of 56 miles per hour (90 kilometres per hour), it does even better – 81 miles per gallon or 29 kilometres per litre. Before the year 2000 we may have a car made of lighter materials and with better aerodynamic design which can do

100 miles to the gallon, or 35 kilometres to the litre.

Cars must also be used efficiently. Low-powered cars may be used for driving in the city, and higher-powered cars hired for travelling between cities. More people will share cars for their journeys. In Istanbul, Khartoum and other Asian and African cities, people have long been sharing minibus-taxis. For one person to be sitting in a car designed for four people is a terrible waste of resources.

Public transport should become more important in the future. Special lanes where only buses can drive could be extended to keep the traffic flowing. Another idea is to allow only certain people to bring their cars into the city centre. Their number plates will have a device which can be read electronically. This scheme could be used to restrict traffic in other areas too.

When oil runs out . . .
Why can we not do away with the gasoline (petrol) engine? Electricity does not pollute the air we breathe. Electric vehicles are clean, quiet and safe: they are already used for specialized purposes, such as milk deliveries.

The trouble is that we have not yet produced cheap, high-performance batteries. The US car firm General Motors has developed a battery-driven car which can reach a top speed of 50 miles per hour (80 kilometres per hour). Its zinc-nickel oxide battery has to be re-charged every 100 miles (160 kilometres) or so. Other firms are experimenting with sodium-sulphur batteries.

Electricity is particularly suitable for commercial vans working within the city. In a world in which microelectronics are completely changing the internal design of the motor car, it seems probable that the battery problem will be solved.

▲ We may all be using these forms of transport in the future. They will be fast (like the monorail) and use a minimum of fuel (like the electric car). Several designs are already in hand for a new airship.

Off the road

This high-speed train in Kyoto, Japan, can carry many people.

A car can transport only four or, if it is big, perhaps six people. The average bus cannot hold much more than forty people. Long ago it was realized that other types of transport would be needed for the modern city, where great masses of people have to get to work and back home again.

The world's first underground railway, London's Metropolitan line, opened in 1863. It used steam engines and carried 9 500 000 passengers in its first year. A single track of a modern electric system, such as that used in Tokyo, can carry over 70 000 passengers an hour. An electric underground system causes no traffic jams, no air pollution, and it takes up very little land on the surface.

City transit schemes
Some cities have rail systems where the tracks are high above the city. Germany has a successful monorail system, in which the carriages are suspended from a single overhead rail. In France a kind of 'hovertrain' – an air-cushioned vehicle which runs on a track – has been used for city transport.

Some of the most successful transit schemes combine two forms of transport. In Cologne and Amsterdam, for example, existing tram systems have been combined with an underground system – the tram simply descends into a tunnel on approaching the city centre. In London and in San Diego light rail systems use the same rail tracks as mainline trains. But the railbus might prove to be the most valuable sign of things to come. The railbus is a bus with rubber tyres which can also travel on steel rails. It should be cheap and efficient.

Suburban travel
We have seen how the electronic revolution may change the way we work. More and more businesses might move away from the centre of the city. Will this mean that underground railways designed to take people to the centre will not be needed by the next century? Some people have suggested this and predicted that more light rail overground trains will be needed to link together communities that today are served by buses and trams.

Whatever happens, unless cheap mass transport is introduced, there is little hope of an alternative to the noisy, unhealthy motor car.

Waterways
Many cities possess old canal systems. In Venice and Amsterdam the waterways were originally the highways of the city. In the future these old canals, at present often strewn with floating garbage, could be used again. Boats can carry heavy freight and, although they will never provide rapid mass transport, canal boats can provide an interesting trip for tourists.

Airports

The skies of our cities are today filled with aircraft taking off and landing at large airports on the outskirts. In some cities helicopters ferry passengers from the airport to a heliport in the city centre. Heliports will almost certainly become more common in future.

◀ A people-mover in Morgantown, West Virginia. It is powered by electricity, has no driver and provides individuals with a small, quiet and clean form of transport. Will it replace the motor car?

The development of vertical take-off and land (VTOL) and short take-off and land (STOL) aircraft means that small airports can be built in inner city areas. One has been suggested for London's former docklands on the Thames.

An STOL plane such as the de Havilland Canada Dash 7, which carries fifty passengers, has very quiet engines and so causes little disturbance. An STOL airport needs a runway of only 2500 feet (760 metres). The range of such a plane is about 400 miles (645 kilometres), so businessmen will be able to get quickly from one city to another for meetings.

▼ A short take-off and land airport has been suggested for London's disused docklands. It would allow business people to fly to within a few miles of the city centre.

Enjoying the city

Pisa in Italy. The streets, squares, and buildings of many old cities are enjoyed not only by the people who live there, but by tourists too.

In looking at the problems of cities it is easy to forget that cities are very often exciting and enjoyable places. While there are slums and traffic jams there are also theatres, concerts, new fashions, amazing buildings, parks and galleries, zoos, cinemas and sporting events.

It is not even necessary to spend money. On the street, buskers, or street performers, stage little plays and comical scenes. For years they were treated as beggars, and are still forbidden to perform in many places. However wherever they have been encouraged – outside the Pompidou Centre in Paris, for example, or in London's Covent Garden, they are a great success.

The streets of cities such as Cairo or Bombay are chaotic, but fascinating to stroll in because so much happens there. The cities of the future should not be made up of empty stretches of concrete, but of bustling streets.

Many nationalities

Any big capital city is exciting too because of the mixture of people who would not otherwise live side by side. People of different race and nationality can meet and learn about each other's customs and beliefs. A New Yorker might be black or white, Italian, Jewish, Irish or Puerto Rican. An inhabitant of Mombasa might be of African, European, Indian or Arabic descent.

A city's shops, markets and restaurants are usually as mixed as its inhabitants. In London you can eat traditional food from all over the world in, for example, Chinese, Indian, French, Italian, American, Jewish, even Russian, Persian, or Japanese restaurants.

Open spaces

Wherever your city might be, you will need parks or gardens to relax in – somewhere to sunbathe, play football or chess, feed the ducks or listen to a band. Central Park in New York and Golden Gate Park in San Francisco are among the most important places to the inhabitants of those cities.

Parks, gardens, rivers and canals may be home to many animals and unusual plants. All kinds of birds nest in the city, attracted by the warmth of the buildings and the lack of predators. Plants and animals soon take over wasteland.

Parks are not the only open spaces people can use. You can walk along canals and rivers or go boating in them. Any square, plaza or wide corner can, with the addition of trees and benches, become a place to relax and talk to people, rather than windy places to hurry through.

Electronic entertainment

The way people enjoy themselves does not change much over the centuries. Plays, fairs, pleasure gardens, wrestling matches and football are enjoyed today as much as they were in medieval cities. The cinema, however, is a 20th century invention, and today the video is turning many

▲ Cities are often exciting and enjoyable. People in Paris may stroll in the streets or sit at café tables watching the world go by.

▶ People enjoy a game of baseball in New York's Central Park.

bars and clubs into mini-cinemas.

The great 'theme-parks', such as Disneyland, developed in the United States, are spreading elsewhere. Computers can now copy human speech and movement with uncanny accuracy. In the electronic age the traditional 'waxwork' can speak and move.

Entertainment is an important part of city life. We shall be making the most of it in 2000!

CHAPTER 6
2000 and beyond

Early in the 20th century planners began to think about controlling the way cities grow and change. Today, city dwellers in most cities in the developed world have some power to affect planning and influence what cities will be like in the year 2000 and later. This is because governments, architects and planners now pay more attention to what people want from city life.

But planning, even careful planning, does not always work well. As we have already seen, the highrise apartment towers built in the 1960s failed and many were torn down. In other words, as planners look for solutions to present problems they may create new ones.

City look-alikes
A problem in the next century could be look-alike cities, places without a clear character of their own. Flying over, say, Hamburg you may look out of the aircraft window and think you're over Chicago, Toronto or Buenos Aires. Already one office skyscraper can look much like another. Could it be that beyond the year 2000 whole areas of the world's cities will have lost their special character? Will taking a holiday in another city be like staying at home?

It *is* possible. As long ago as 1929, two planners in America called Hitchcock and Johnson said problems of city design all over the world could be solved in the same way. Today, university buildings in Libya, Peking and Mexico look very similar. Holiday Inns and Hilton hotels built in places as different as Bali, Cincinnati, Alaska and Lagos are designed to be identical. People visiting these luxury hotels know exactly what standard of service to expect there.

▶ Is it possible that cities in the future could begin to look the same? Soon this big city could be anywhere in the world. Even products advertised on billboards could be the same the world over.

Look-alike shopping
In most European cities today you can visit a busy shopping street and call at different individual shops. They specialize in one particular line – anything from clothes to fishing tackle, from handmade sweets to sea food or do-it-yourself equipment. Each shop has its own character.

In many parts of America, Canada, South Africa, Mexico, Australia and Brazil a very different system is popular. You may go to one or two big department stores and get everything you need. Or you may go to a special shopping plaza or complex built on several floors. This makes shopping quicker and easier because everything you want is in there somewhere. But it may also be boring. You may have less choice in what to buy because goods for sale become standardized.

Multinationals – big companies with branches and offices all over the world – already sell products such as Coca Cola and tape recorders everywhere, from the jungles of Indonesia to the Arctic Circle.

In future, driving from any airport to any city we may see roadside billboards advertising the same products. The skyline may look like any city anywhere. The airport too may look like those in other countries, and when we reach the city itself we may find the same fast-food companies and restaurants, but few traditional local shops.

Standardized people
Could people become more alike if goods and architecture are standardized? Travellers through the ages have gone on journeys not only to see places but different people and customs. But today's newspapers and television describe the latest ideas, fashions and dances to the whole world. You can see the same film in New York and Harare. Tomorrow, then, we may dress and think more alike than ever before. Preserving our traditional character and local customs could become an important matter.

53

Communities in action

In the next century different cities may look more alike. They may become cold, unfriendly places where people feel dwarfed by concrete and stone. But we may reject this possibility and instead work for cities with a human face, where people feel involved in the changing life around them. In even the biggest world capitals today there are many communities of people who feel they belong together and can work as a group on local problems.

Tenants take control
A housing estate in Jersey City in America had such a bad reputation for drugs and crime that tenants were afraid to tell others that they lived there. Lifts did not work, light bulbs were not replaced, stairs were cluttered with garbage, people threw their garbage out of the windows. Crime was so bad police set up a station on the estate. Instead of this helping, the crime rate went up higher.

Finally, the tenants formed a committee to take on the problems themselves, rather than wait for outside help. They appointed captains to guard each floor and elevator. The whole place was repaired and cleaned up inside and out. Grass and flowers were planted outside.

This worked so well tenants went further and set up a parent-teachers association so parents could talk to teachers at the local school about their children's work. People began to be proud of living on the estate. Some of the tasks tenants had taken on were made into full-time paid jobs for the unemployed. This self-help system spread to other housing estates where tenants successfully took up the fight against crime and slum conditions.

In Islington, London, people persuaded the local council to repair old houses and give them to a society especially formed by the tenants. Through membership of this society they owned the houses jointly. Fine old buildings which were turning into slums were saved thanks to group effort by local people.

Village in the city
Small communities within the big city are not created only by people fighting problems together. Many cities have village-like areas. Some of these actually were villages in the open countryside before the city grew up around them.

A population of about 50 000 to 100 000 people is just right for the urban village. If they are smaller than this, they may not be able to fight builders or planners who want to change the area.

Planners can be on the side of community life or the urban village. Evry is a French satellite town (see page 29) created to draw people and industry away from overcrowded Paris. It has a specially built town centre with sports facilities, dance halls,

◀ Places where people can meet and enjoy themselves help to make community spirit stronger.

theatres, social centres and a library. All this is meant to help people enjoy their leisure together.

Les Halles in Paris and Covent Garden in London were two areas with a strong community life and spirit. Both contained produce markets which were so busy they created severe traffic problems. Plans to tear them down and replace them with highrise offices were rejected in Paris and London. People knew the skyscrapers would destroy the community, so they fought for schemes which included houses for poorer people and which allowed small businesses to flourish there.

Shanty villages
In big Third World cities no one worries about shanty towns (see pages 20 and 21) losing their character. Providing housing and services for these gigantic areas is the main problem. But again self-help, along with government aid, has been seen as a solution, at least for the time being.

Instead of bulldozing shanties, city councils should lay on water and sewerage. They should allow people to remain and help them build their own houses by providing materials, or money to buy materials. And they should make sure that there is land for poorer families to live on legally. So far only a few cities such as Dar es Salaam in Tanzania, Lusaka in Zambia, Lima in Peru and Khartoum in the Sudan have done this to any great extent.

▲ People in Africa often build their own houses with simple materials. Governments are encouraged to supply cheap materials to shanty-town dwellers.

▼ An adventure playground in London, built on waste-ground by the local community.

Fact or fantasy?

Scientific research has helped us to understand much of the Universe. We can look ahead beyond 2000 to a time when we can begin to conquer space and perhaps set up perfect artificial cities in the sky. Science will rescue present cities from whatever problems trouble them now. Or will it? Is it really as easy as that? Can we leave everything to modern technology and hope for the best?

Perhaps not. Science, particularly medical science, has helped make the world a lot safer and easier for many people. But our cities and the world have never been in greater danger of total destruction through nuclear war. Science has given us great power but everything depends on how we use it.

Rich world, poor world
While people in the cities of the developed world reap the rewards of technological progress, people in Third World cities have to struggle to survive. Not only that but the wealth of the developed world rests squarely on the poverty of the Third World. Rich countries use raw materials from poor ones to create manufactured goods. They don't pay prices high enough to really enrich the poor nations. Then they sell the manufactured goods back to them at high prices. So there is a rich world and a poor world.

As we saw on pages 12 and 13, we already have the ability to feed many of the world's starving people by farming cereals. But because the rich world wants to eat beef steak and hamburgers, cattle is farmed instead. In other words, we may have solutions to world problems but choose not to use them.

A city in space
While Third World shanty towns grow and grow, exciting plans have been discussed to build a city in space. It might soon be

possible. A tube will rotate around a central hub fast enough to create an effect of gravity, keeping land and water firmly in place. There might be a solar power station to create energy for use inside the tube. Louvred windows would control the amount of sunshine and perpetual sun would allow farmers to grow several crops a year. There could be grass, lakes, water, trees, birds and animals living in a perfect artificial environment.

It sounds like science fiction come true, but who would really gain from it? Only the rich would be able to use it. And the people who would gain most from it are the already-rich companies who would build it. They are the ones who want the US Government to take the idea seriously.

The real choices for the future are whether we want faceless cities or more human ones. Do we want to spend money on social problems? Do we want armies and weapons, or hospitals and aid for the poor? Does the rich world want to stay rich at the expense of the poor world, even though in the long-run it will not be able to survive unless the balance of wealth across the globe is made more fair?

Remember that if these problems were easy to solve they wouldn't be there at all.

Although we cannot predict the future it is not foolish to feel hopeful about 2000 and beyond. In recent times people have become more concerned about planning a good future. A lot of cities are good places to live in for most people. Even in the Third World people come off the land to shanty towns looking for a better life. Usually they find it. In 2000 cities may be better still.

A city built in space would create its own atmosphere and gravity. It would also cost a lot and benefit only the rich. Do we want it while so many of the world's people are poor?

Glossary

Aerodynamics A branch of science which studies air or other gases in motion. A machine that is aerodynamically designed moves easily through the air. It needs less fuel and is cheaper to run.

Aid Help or support. A rich country may offer aid to a poor country – money, surplus food or workers. Central or local government may offer aid to a particular region or district within their own country.

Allotment A plot of public land where city dwellers who have no garden may apply to grow vegetables, etc.

Architecture The design and planning of buildings, and the buildings themselves.

Avenue A broad city street often lined with trees.

Busker A street entertainer who often asks for payment from passers-by.

Canal An artificial waterway. Before railways were developed canals were often important for moving goods to and between cities.

Capital The city which contains the government of a nation. Bonn is the capital of West Germany.

Capitalism A system of economics in which most businesses or factories are privately owned.

Central government The body of people who run a country. Cities are usually governed partly by central government and partly by a city government.

Cereals Name for members of the grass family such as wheat, oats, rye and rice which are important items in our diet.

Communications Ways of sending and receiving information: telephones, postal services, radio and television are examples.

Communism A way of organizing society in which all or most property is publicly or communally owned.

Community Any group of people having something in common – often used to describe people living in the same place.

Commuter Somebody who regularly travels into the city to work and then returns to the suburbs or another town or the country.

Conservation Saving things. Old buildings may be 'conserved' by not pulling them down to make way for new buildings; fuel may be 'conserved' by preventing waste, loss of heat, etc.

Council A body of people chosen for a special purpose such as helping to organize and govern a city.

Density A measure of the concentration of something in a given area or volume, for example, a measure of the people or buildings within a given area.

Developed country A relatively rich country with most of its inhabitants in towns or cities and with a large industrial output.

Dockland The area of a port surrounding the wharves (where ships load and unload their cargoes).

Downtown An American term for that part of the city which forms the centre of business and entertainment.

Energy A source of power. Burning coal, gas, and oil releases energy which can heat buildings or power machinery (like cars or factory production lines). Wind and the Sun's rays also are sources of energy.

Estate An area of town specially developed for housing or for factories.

Factory A building or buildings where goods are manufactured.

Flyover A section of a road which is raised to cross over other roads or buildings.

Fossil fuel Remains of plant and animal life from millions of years ago which today can provide sources of **energy**. Examples are coal, oil and natural gas.

Garden City A city which has been carefully planned for industry and homes with many open spaces to make it more pleasant to live there.

Generator A machine for producing electricity. It can be driven by burning coal or oil to produce steam which drives the generator, or by 'falling water' in a dam.

Graffiti Drawings or words defacing public buildings or transport.

Green belt An area of countryside surrounding a city, where building is forbidden or limited by law.

Grid pattern A very ancient form of city planning used in some of the earliest cities thousands of years ago. It was popular in the United States. A series of straight roads form a criss-cross network, with the buildings in blocks of a standard length.

Heat pump When used for heating a house, a heat pump extracts heat from the air or ground outside, compresses it (which makes it hotter) and releases it inside.

Heliport A place for helicopters to land and take off.

Highrise Tall (of buildings). Highrise buildings provide a great deal of space for offices or flats within a small area, but are not always pleasant to live in.

Hydroponics The science of growing plants without soil, the plants being fed by chemicals.

Industrial Revolution A great change in society when more and more people came to live in cities and work in factories or city-based businesses rather than agriculture. It took place first in Britain in the late 18th and early 19th centuries and many Western nations followed soon after. There are still many countries, especially in Africa and Asia, which have not gone through a similar process and where most people still work in agriculture and live in the countryside.

Industry Production of goods (often called **manufacture**) in a factory. Heavy industry is the manufacture of large-scale machinery or metal products, eg shipbuilding. Light industry is the manufacture or processing of small items, eg food-canning.

Inner city Central part of a city, often the oldest part. Some of it may be rundown. See **slum**.

Insulation Material used to prevent heat or electricity passing through something. Insulation in walls or the loft of a house will reduce the amount of heat lost from a house and lower fuel bills in winter.

Internal combustion engine Engine in which fuel is burnt inside the engine to make a piston go in and out. This movement is used to drive machinery such as cars and trucks.

Light rail A short-distance city or suburban railway, designed to carry passengers.

Lowrise Of buildings, limited to a few storeys only.

Malnutrition Being unhealthy due to lack of enough food and/or the right kind of food.

Manufacture The making of goods for sale, either by human labour or by machinery.

Megacity A city of gigantic size, or with a very large population.

Microchip See **silicon chip**.

Microelectronics The use of miniature electronic circuits, largely developed in the 1970s and 1980s. It is transforming manufacture and employment.

Microwaves Electromagnetic waves of extremely high frequency. They can be used to cook food very quickly in a special oven. They can also be used to transmit information along a beam between two places.

Migration The movement of people from one place (country, city or area) to another.

Mixed economy An economic system in which some firms are owned privately, and others are owned by the state.

Monorail A railway whose carriages travel on a single (normally overhead) rail.

Multinational company A company which has factories or offices in many different countries.

Municipal Connected with city government.

New Town A city which has been specially built from scratch: an example is Milton Keynes in England.

Ocean City A plan developed in Japan to build a city on the sea.

Office A workplace where people do not manufacture things but provide services or information. For example, people who work for banks, insurance companies or for government work in offices.

Open space Part of a city without buildings, such as a park.

Outskirts The outer edge of a town or city.

Photovoltaic cell A cell which can turn sunlight straight into electricity; it can be used in water-heating systems etc.

Planning City or town planning is the control of the way in which cities develop. It is usually organized by city government.

Pollution The poisoning of the environment by smoke, dirt, sewage, chemicals, industrial waste etc.

Population The number of people living in a given area. In order to keep an accurate record, a 'census' or count is carried out at regular intervals in most nations and cities.

Power station A factory or building which generates electricity by using steam power or the power of falling water (controlled by a dam) to drive a turbine-generator. See **generator**.

Private sector Those firms in a mixed economy which are privately owned.

Protein One of the most essential parts of our food.

Public sector Those firms or services in a mixed economy which are owned or controlled by the public or the State.

Railbus A road bus which is designed to run along rails for part of its journey.

Rates Taxes on property, raised by local governments in many countries. They are used to pay for things like water supplies and garbage collection.

Raw materials Unprocessed substances for use in **manufacture,** eg iron ore.

Recycling The use of wastes as raw material in making new materials. For instance, waste aluminium cans or paper or glass can be reprocessed so the material is used again and not just thrown away.

Reservoir A place where water is stored for public use.

Resources Useful material for doing or making things, eg iron, fertile land, forests, or money.

Robot A machine which can be programmed to do work traditionally carried out by humans.

Rural Belonging to or in the countryside.

Satellite town A town on the **outskirts** of a city which has its own centre with shops, although many of its residents still go to work in the main city.

Service industry A business which sells services – eg banking, insurance – instead of goods.

Shanty town An area of makeshift housing, such as huts and shacks which house many of the people of Third World cities. Such developments are unplanned and often illegal.

Silicon chip (also microchip) A tiny chip of silicon into which is squeezed all the components and interconnections of an electronic computer. Making this ever smaller, more powerful and cheaper is the key to the electronics revolution of the 1970s and 1980s.

Skyscraper Any very tall building. The Sears Tower in Chicago is 1454 feet (443 metres) high.

Slum A poor district or building, run down and in bad repair. Slums are usually older buildings near the city centre.

Smog A word made up from 'smoke' and 'fog'. Pollution of the air by factories or motor traffic.

Solar panel There are two types, one which converts sunlight into electricity (see **photovoltaic cell**). The other type can capture some of the sun's heat and use it to provide hot water or heat for rooms.

Space city A plan for a city to be constructed in space.

Squatters People who occupy buildings or land illegally.

State A nation or its government. A state-owned (nationalized) industry is owned by the public and run on behalf of the government. Some nations are divided into 'states', so in this case a 'state government' controls an area smaller than the nation.

STOL Short Take-Off and Land: a kind of aircraft which does not need long runways.

Suburb An outlying part of town.

Tax A sum of money demanded from individuals or businesses by government. It is applied to income, purchases, and to imports of certain goods (for example, cigarettes, petrol and alcoholic drinks are often heavily taxed), and is used for funding government activities.

Tenant Someone who rents the property they occupy.

Third World The poorer countries, particularly those which do not belong to the large capitalist or communist blocs of the northern half of the world. Three quarters of the world's population live in the Third World.

Tower block A skyscraper or highrise building.

Unemployment Lack of work: a growing problem in the cities of the 1980s.

Urban To do with the city (from the Latin word *urbs*, 'city').

Utopia A dream or vision of some perfect place or trouble-free society. *Utopia* was the title of a book written by Sir Thomas More in 1516. In ancient Greek the title means 'nowhere'.

Vandalism The pointless destruction or damage of public property.

Ventilation Way of providing fresh air in an enclosed space.

VTOL Vertical Take-Off and Land: a kind of aircraft which needs no runway – it goes straight up and down.

Workforce People employed or available for employment.

Worksharing The practice of more than one person sharing the same job on a part-time basis.

Zoning The division of a city into special planning areas. Some areas may be zoned just for homes or just for industry, for instance.

Index

Picture acknowledgements

BBC Hulton Picture Library 27 top
Camerapix Hutchison 2 bottom, 4 top left, 6 centre, 14, 21 bottom, 34, 48 bottom, 50-51 **J. Allan Cash Photolibrary** 4 bottom, 6-7, 13 bottom, 37 **Daily Telegraph Colour Library** 1, 7, 23 top, 35 left, 35 centre, 35 right **Mary Evans Picture Library** 27 bottom **Explorer** 42 top inset **Finnish Tourist Board** 28 bottom left **The Guardian** 31 **Robert Harding Picture Library** 6 top, 6 bottom, 9 bottom, 16 top, 20, 21 top, 54 **Illustrated London News Picture Library** 49 **Inter-Action Trust** 55 bottom **London Transport** 17 **The Mansell Collection** 16 bottom **Milton Keynes Development Corporation** 28 top **Multimedia Publications** 42 centre left inset **NASA** 3, 56-57 **Photographers' Library** 9 top, 23 bottom, 51 **The Photo Source** 26 bottom, 45 **Photri** 22 top, 48 top **Rex Features** 42 left **Site Projects, New York** 4 centre, 30 top **Frank Spooner Pictures** 30 bottom **UNICEF** 55 top **The Venice in Peril Fund** 33 **Vision International** 28 bottom right, 42 centre right inset **ZEFA** 2 top, 4 top right, 13 top, 19, 24, 26 top, 29, 32, 42 bottom inset, 43 top inset, 43 bottom left inset, 43 bottom right inset, 43, 44, 50

Artwork by **Mulkern Rutherford** and **John Strange**

Multimedia Publications (UK) Limited have endeavoured to observe the legal requirements with regard to the suppliers of photographic illustrative materials.

Page numbers in *italics* refer to relevant illustrations and captions.

Abuja 46
aircraft *13*, 49, *49*
air pollution 46, 48
airports 49, *49*, 53
Akkad 17
Amsterdam 43, 48
Antwerp 17
Arcosanti 30, *30*
Athens 17
Atlanta 35

beggary 19, 50
Berlin *42*, 43
Bombay 10, *21*, 50
Boston 10
Bournville 27
Brasilia 29, *29*
Bronx *22*
Bruges 17
Buenos Aires 52
Buffalo 34
building materials 36
buses 10, *11*, 12, 17, 20, 48
busking 50
bus lanes 47

Cadbury, George 27
Cairo *14*, *15*, 50
Calcutta 13, 20
canals 48, 50
Canberra 29
cars *11*, 12, 46–7, 48
  electric 46, 47
central heating 41
Chicago 34, 35, 52
Cincinnati 52
cinemas 50–51
cities:
  advantages 18
  building of 34–41
  capital 29
  centres *11*
  conservation 32
  design 24, 52
  disadvantages 18, 50
  electricity 12, *13*
  employment 18–19, 20, *21*, *42*, *43*, 44–5
  food 12–13, *13*, 20
  fuel 12
  futuristic 30–31, *30*, *31*
  gas 12, *13*
  governments 11; *see also* councils
  health care 18
  in history 16–19, 26–7
  huge 20–21
  industrial 18, *19*
  inner 22
  life in 10, 42–51
  look-alike 52–3, *52*, 54
  manufactured goods 12
  nature 10–11
  new 28–9
  old 18, *19*, 22–3, 24, *24*
  open spaces 24, 50
  planning 24–33, 34, 52
  populations 8, 10, 18, 20
  repairs 23

sewerage 15, *15*, 17, 23, 55
  in space 56–7, *56–7*
  spreading 25, *25*
  starvation 18
  supplying 12–13
  Third World 13, 18–21, *19*, 42, 55, 56, 57
  transport 8, 10, 12, 46–9, *47*, 48
  underground 34, 37, *37*
  walled 24, 26
  waste-removal 14–15, *15*
  water 12, *13*, *15*
clean air laws 15, 24
climate, artificial *31*
coal 12
Cologne 48
communications 13
  see also newspapers; radio; telephones; television
communications satellites 13
community spirit 21, 34, 54–5, *55*
commuting *44*
computers 8, 17, 44, *44*, *45*, 51
  central 41
  home (micro-) 41, *41*
conservation areas 32
corporations *see* councils
councils 11, 20, 22, 25, *43*
Covent Garden *23*, 50, 55
crime 22, *22*, 29, 34, 54
Cumbernauld 29
Cuzco 32

Dar es Salaam 55
disease 18
Disneyland 51
drought 18
drug abuse 54

electricity 12, *13*, 20, 39, 41, 47
electricity supplies 10
elevators 34
employment 18–19, 20, *21*, *42*, *43*, 44–5
energy 12, 38, 39
energy-conservation houses 38–9, *39*
entertainment 45, 50–51
Evry 54–5
exhaust fumes 46

factories 19, 20, 22, 25, 44
farming (agriculture) 13, 16, *19*, 45, 56
fireproofing 34
fish farming 13, *13*
flyovers 46
food 12–13, *13*, 20
fossil fuels 38
France 28–9, 48, 54–5
fuel 12, 38
fusion power 12

gadgets, household 12, 41
Garden Cities 27, 28, *28*
gardens, public 50
gas 12, *13*
gasoline 12, 46
governments:
  central 11, 20–21, 25, 39, 45, 52
  city 11; *see also* councils
  Third World 19, 20–21
Green Belts 25, *25*, *29*
grid pattern 24, *24*

Hamburg 52
Harare 53
Haussmann, Georges-Eugène, Baron 27
heating 12, 38
heat-trap houses 38–9, *39*
heliports 49
Helsinki *28*, 29
highrise buildings 34, *34*, *35*, 36, 52, 55
  see also skyscrapers
Hitler, Adolf 32
homes (houses) 36, 38–41, *41*
  electronic 41
  heat-trap 38–9, *39*
Hong Kong *13*, 34
hospitals 11, 57
household gadgets *see* gadgets
hovertrains 48
Howard, Ebenezer 27, 28
hydrogen fusion 12
hydroponics 12
hydropower 12

Incas 32
Industrial Revolution *16*, 17, *17*, 18, 21, 22, 25
industry 17, 18, 25
  changing 23
  machines for 12
  manufacturing 10, 44, *45*
  service 44, *45*
  State-run 10-11
Indus Valley 26, *26*
insulation 38, 39
Islington 54
Istanbul 43, 47

Japan 31, *31*, 44, 48
Jersey City 54
job sharing 45

Khartoum 47, 55
Kish 17
kitchen gadgets *see* gadgets
Kyoto *48*

Lagos 13, 20, 46, 52
land shortages 34
Latin America 19
lead 46
leisure 45
Les Halles *22*, 55
Letchworth 28
Lever, William, 1st Viscount Leverhulme 27
lifts 34
light 24, 25
lighting 12
Lima 10, 55
London 23, 32, 48, 49, *49*, 55
  character 43
  Green Belts around 25
  growth of 17, *17*
  markets *13*, *22*, *23*, 50, 55
  New Towns around 29
  population 17
  slums *16*, 54
  squatting 43
  tower blocks *35*
Los Angeles 46

lowrise buildings 34, 36–7, *37*
Lusaka 55

Machu Picchu 32
Manhattan 24, *31*, 34
manufactured goods 12
manufacturing industries 10, 44, *45*
medicine 18, 56
megacities 20–21, *21*
Mexico 26, *26*, 52
Mexico City 10, 18, 46
microchips 41
microelectronics 44, *47*
Milan 10
Milton Keynes *28*
minibus-taxis 47
Mohenjo-daro 26, *26*
Mombasa 50
monorail systems 48
Montreal 37
More, Sir Thomas 27, *27*
Morgantown *49*
Moscow 25
multinational companies 53

New Lanark 27
newspapers 10, 13, 44, *45*, 53
New Towns *17*, 28–9
New York 13, 18, *19*, 24, *31*, *35*, 50, *51*, 53
    character 43
    crime *22*
    domestic waste *15*
    early skyscrapers 34
    traffic jams 25
noise 22, 25
nuclear war 37, 56

Ocean City 30, 31, *31*
offices 10, 19, 23, 34, 44
oil 12, 46
Olinda *21*
open spaces 24, 50
overcrowding 18, 20
overspill 28
Owen, Robert 27

Paris 50, *51*, 54
    character 43
    growth 28–9
    highrise apartments 34
    markets *22*, 55
    redesign of 27, *27*
parks 50
Peking 26, 52
people-movers *49*
Perth (Australia) *37*
petrol 12, 46
photovoltaic cells 39
Pisa *50*
Pittsburgh 25
pollution 15, *15*, 46, 48
populations:
    city 8, 10, 18, 20, 28
    growth 18, 25
    London's 17
    overspill 28
    world 10
Port Sunlight 27
poverty *16*, 18, 21, 23, 42, 56, 57

power failures 20
power stations 12
private sector 10–11
public sector 10–11
public transport 46, 47

radio 10, 13
railbuses 48
rates 22
    see also taxes
recycling 14, *14*, 15
rents *21*, 22
reservoirs 12
ring roads 46
Rio de Janeiro 20, 43
rivers 12, 50
roads 11, *16*, 23, 46
robots 41, 44
Rome *14*, 17, 34, 43
rubbish *see* waste
rubbish collection 11, 15

San Diego 48
San Francisco 50
Sargon *16*, 17
satellites, artificial 13
satellite towns 28, 54
schools 11, 18
seaports 17
Seine River 29
service industries 44, *45*
sewage 15, *15*, 21
sewage farms 15, *15*
sewers 14, *15*, 17, 23, 55
shanty towns 20–21, *21*, 22, 29, 43, 55, *55*, 56, 57
shopping centres 23, 36, 37, 53
silicon chips 41
skyscrapers 8, 16, 17, 34, *35*, 36, 42, 52
    building of 34, *35*
    complete cities in *30*
    early 34
slavery 17
slums *16*, 18, 20, 21, 22, 23, 50, 54
smog 46
smoke *16*, 25
solar panels 38–9
solar power 12, 38–9, 57
Soleri, Paolo 30
squatting *42*, 43
Stockholm 29
street cleaning 10
street festivals *21*
streets 24
suburbs *16*, 17, *17*, 22, 36, *37*

Tapiola *28*, 29
taxes 10, 11, 28
television 13, 41, 53
Teotihuacan 26, *26*
Thames River 23, 49
Third World:
    cities in 13, 18–21, *19*, 42, 55, 56, 57
    governments 19
    houses 36
Tokyo 25, *29*, 48
Toronto 52
tower blocks 34
    see also highrise buildings; skyscrapers

trade 16, 17, 26
traffic jams 25, 28, 46, 48, 50
trains (railways) *11*, 13, *13*, *16*, 17, 20, 29, 44, 48, *48*
    modernization 45
trams 48
transport 8, 10, 12, 46–9, *47*
    see also aircraft; buses; cars; trains
Troy 14–15

underground cities 34, 37, *37*
underground railways 48
unemployment 22, 23, 29, 44–5
universities 11, 52
Ur *16*, 17
urban expressways 46
urban sprawl *see* cities (spreading)
urban villages 54
Utopia 27, *27*

vandalism *22*
Venice 32, *33*, 48
ventilation 34, 38–9
videos 8, 41, 45, 50–51
Vienna 43
villages 17, 19, *19*
violence 22

walled cities 24, 26
Warsaw 32, *32*
Washington DC 29
waste:
    disposal 20; *see also* rubbish collection
    domestic (rubbish) 14–15, *15*, 21
    heat 38
    human 14, 15; *see also* sewage
    industrial 14, 15
water 12, *13*, 17, 20, 21, 23, 55
waterways 48
Watt, James 17
wave-power 12
weapons 57
wells 12, 20
Westvaco 15
wind-power 12, 39
work *see* employment
working week 45
World War Two 22, 32, *32*

Yokohama *29*

Zabaleen *14*
zoning 25, *25*, 26

Robinson Township Library
Robinson, Illinois 62454